M|S|T|J · FAMINU

01|09
990

GW00492898

"Driven by discontent with life commonly lived in two separate worlds (spiritual and business), Daryl Kraft is unwilling to shrink from the claims of Christ in all dimensions of his life. *The Businessman's Guide* chronicles experiences that have fueled Daryl's passion for Christ-honoring excellence in business and integrity of heart."

Dr. Dennis Dirks, Dean
Talbot School of Theology, California

"Through Daryl's sharing of God's wisdom and work in his life, I have come to love my life, my wife, my career, and most of all, Jesus. No other man, in my time, has had more impact upon my spiritual life, my marriage, my career, and my ministry to others. If you're not loving life, find a quiet place, a box of tissues, open this book, and prepare your heart for some exploratory surgery."

Jonathan Hanks
Environment Control Franchisee, Ohio

"Over the years I have met many men in athletics, in ministry, and in the business world. I've known very few with the integrity and commitment to blend Jesus Christ into their environment with more dedication than Daryl Kraft. I highly recommend the blessings you'll receive from the insights in *The Businessman's Guide to Real Success*. You'll glean from the life and years that Daryl has walked with his Lord through every phase of his life."

Rev. John Werhas, Pastor
Evangelical Free Church, California,
former Dodger

"Daryl is someone in whom the Scriptures breathe. Again and again he has taught me the power of God's Word to change lives. His story is exciting, because I've experienced it and know it to be true."

John Lamb
Environment Control Franchisee, Wisconsin

"As a staff member who has been associated with Daryl for more than 25 years, I've witnessed firsthand the amazing changes God has brought about—first in his personal life, then in his family life, then in staff relationships, and, ultimately, in the day-to-day life of the business. I feel this book will have lasting value and become a resource companion of encouragement to others on their own journey of genuine freedom in Christ."

Richard Shirk, Vice President
Environment Control, California

"The life-changing truths that God has given to Daryl in this book have given me the handles in life to be the husband, father, and businessman God desires. Nothing else has impacted my life in such a way as these life-giving truths from God's Word."

Ben Evans
Environment Control Franchisee, California

"Having been closely associated with the Kraft family and the business, Environment Control, as its corporate counsel for 27 years, I can testify to the accuracy and truth in Daryl's words. This book is not only a testimony to the life of a 'struggling' Christian, it is a book for non-Christians, who can find in its writings a sense of the Christian faith."

Charles Ermes
Attorney, California

"This book is a must for men. Daryl describes, through his personal experiences, the application of God's truth in his personal life, his marriage, his family, and his business. After almost 30 years as a business colleague, I know that he 'walks his talk.'"

Nimrod McNair, President
McNair Associates, Inc., Georgia
Chairman, Executive Leadership Foundation, Inc.

"In knowing Daryl for 18 years as a business associate and friend, I can say that this book is an honest and vulnerable account of a man's journey through life, who learns how to exchange his anxieties in his business and family life for God's peace and joy. It can be so confusing and tiring with so many books and seminars on how to be successful in life. It is refreshing to read how Daryl discovered, through his difficult circumstances, how simple it is to be set free from the bondages and lies of sin that so easily entangle each of us, to having a life that's worth living based on the truth of God's character."

Stephen Bryant
Environment Control Franchisee, N. Carolina

"Daryl Kraft is a man that walks his talk. This is a book you will read and read again."

Terry Gniffke, President
Caliber Home Services, Inc., California

The Businessman's Guide to Real Success

by

Daryl Kraft

Bridge-Logos *Publishers*

North Brunswick, NJ

The Businessman's Guide to Real Success
by Daryl Kraft
ISBN 0-88270-744-2
Library of Congress Catalog Card Number: 97-73692
Copyright ©1997 by Daryl Kraft

Published by:
Bridge-Logos *Publishers*
North Brunswick Corporate Center
1300 Airport Road, Suite E
North Brunswick, NJ 08902-1700

Table of Contents

Acknowledgements

My thanks to these editors:

Norm Rohrer: for chunking out the chapters and encouraging me to publish.

Ken Durham: for all the hours extracting the process.

Hollee Chadwick-Loney: for causing Him to increase, and me to decrease.

I also want to express appreciation to these senior employees:

Sharon Patterson: for getting me started.
(Senior Executive Secretary - 15 years)

Karen Dirks: for proofing the manuscript 70x7 times.
(Assistant Executive Secretary - 12 years)

Richard Shirk: for helping me put meat on the bones.
(Vice President - 25 years)

To

Sherryl

my loving and loyal wife,

devoted mother of our children,

faithful servant of God.

Foreword

The Businessman's Guide to Real Success is the story of one man's journey to freedom. In that sense, we could easily call this work a *travelogue*. Daryl has recorded for us a journal of the often treacherous and heart-poundingly rigorous road that lead him to a full realization of what it means to truly be a Christian *and* a succesful businessman.

Daryl discovered, sometimes painfully, that men are men, women are women, kids are people too, right is right, wrong is wrong (and ne'er the twain shall meet), and—the foundation of all bottom lines—*God is God.*

A road map shows you the direction you must go and the route you must take in order to reach your destination. It also highlights the toll roads, scenic highways, shortcuts, and rest stops. It is our desire that this book will serve the same purpose in your business, personal, and spiritual journeys.

And, if along the way a story or two makes you laugh, or cry, then that's a bonus.

During the editorial phase of *The Businessman's Guide to Real Success*, I have logged many hours of conversation with Daryl Kraft. As a former manager with an international service corporation, I have been able to look back and reflect on the difference Daryl's book could have made in my employee and customer relations. Even now, Daryl's experiences and lessons-learned have made a positive impact in my family relationships. Not only have I been able to utilize the knowledge gained from this book, I have also been able to see my spouse's emotions, intentions, and abilities more clearly.

And, guess what?

I'm a woman.

Go figure.

I highly recommend *The Businessman's Guide to Real Success* to every woman who loves a businessman.

In football terms, it's kind of like reading the other teams' play book!

Hollee Chadwick-Loney
Editor, Bridge-Logos Publishers

Introduction

I've cut my teeth—thirty-four years to date—in the business world. I know the gains and losses. I know the challenges, stresses, and disappointments. I also know what it feels like to believe happiness will come from working harder every day at getting ahead.

I had no clue I was just sinking deeper into a world belief system that could never satisfy.

Several years ago we made a decision to build our own Corporate Office Building instead of signing another lease. Our desire was to plan and control our future work environment. We met first with an architect on the exterior and interior design. As the project progressed, the building far exceeded our dreams.

One day while sitting in the architect's office, I said to myself, *God forbid that any of my descendants ever look at this new building and the business it contains and conclude that this is what made me happy.*

That was the seed thought for writing this book. I want to leave a legacy to my future family of what God has done for me.

Because I've been there, chasing that illusive peace for so many years, I also want to encourage men everywhere to commit their lives to REAL success. Then too, I have a deep empathy for wives. I realize today that as long as our male pride justifies our career goals ("I'm doing this for her—to offer her a better life."), it continues to blind us to our total self-centeredness, insensitivity, and preoccupation. While believing we're doing good, our cast iron skillet personalities just continue to shatter our fine china mates.

So to all wives of men like me, I want to say, *you are not alone.* If God can change me, there is hope for your husband. Continue to pray earnestly, and believe that God may someday use you to revolutionize your home.

I've discovered that the world's success, excitement, and fun pale in comparison to the freedom and fulfillment that comes from truly knowing the Lord.

Daryl Kraft

Roots vs. Fruits

"If I can achieve the next plateau in life where my income feels more secure, my kids show me more respect, customers don't complain, employees don't let me down, and nothing else threatens my success—I'll be happier."

That's what I really believed until I saw a young man dying with a painful cancer, having nothing that I had, but everything I wanted—peace! I thought, *"If he has a quiet spirit in circumstances far worse than mine, apparently it is a peace that cannot be achieved or accomplished by anything I have been doing."*

Since this young man's death, the Lord has continued to show me through His Word that peace comes to our lives in the same way apples grow on trees. The apple tree's focus is on sending its roots into the soil for nourishment; and the golden, delicious fruit of peace just appears. As Galatians 5:22 tells us, *" . . . the fruit of the Spirit . . .peace!"*

Now I understand why I didn't know peace for most of my life. I was focused on the fruit end instead of the root end.

—D.K.

1

Dead End

Freedom from Remaining the Same

When God the Father, with glorious power, brought him back to life again, you were given his wonderful new life to enjoy.

Romans 6:4 (TLB)

The view from my office window this morning is spectacular—blue sky, white clouds, and rolling southern California hills. Quietly, with wonder, I think of all that has transpired over the past thirty years. In 1963 my wife and I started what has become a successful nationwide business. However, that's not the source of my amazement. You see, 20 years ago I required tranquilizers just to cope with the anxiety that same business produced. Back then, I was so stressed out I didn't think I could go on. Today, however, I know with complete assurance that I am in the place of God's purpose and calling. More important, I have begun to experience the gift of peace Jesus promised to give those who know Him, a peace that has absolutely nothing to do with the ups and downs of my daily business. In fact, this experience of freedom is the reason for the wonder in my life.

1973

I was in my early thirties and had already achieved what many might consider "the American dream." I had been the owner of a small but growing business for about 10 years, and was president of my own corporation. I lived in a lovely new home on a secluded acre, and was able to drive and replace cars whenever it suited me. My beautiful wife and I had three wonderful, energetic children, and we were all deeply involved in our church. For recreation I hunted big game throughout North America and fished the best streams.

That was me: happy, successful, self-assured, secure. A facade. Those closest to me knew a different me. They knew a person who was quick to anger, uptight, and defensive.

> **Enough was never enough.**

Nothing seemed to satisfy. My wife and I labored two years to build a new house; but six months after we moved in I was so restless and dissatisfied I suggested we sell it and build a bigger one. Though Sherryl made our home an attractive and wonderful refuge, I nagged her and the children about doing better at anything and everything they tried. One stain on the carpet or dead spot in the lawn could ruin my whole day, and therefore, theirs.

Even when I tried to get away to relax, my hunting and fishing pursuits were always overshadowed by a constant feeling that my accomplishments weren't secure enough, big enough, or good enough. As soon as I tackled one feat, I was compelled to outdo it. I was compulsively driven to be something, do something, accomplish something more and better.

The deepening shadows of night often brought worry about my acceptability before God as I fearfully pondered my final destiny. I chewed my fingernails to the quick as I struggled with the stress of maintaining my facade. Often I wondered how I could be a "Christian" and yet be so miserable. I even remember waking my wife in a panic one night and asking, "Have you ever wondered if you are really saved?"

Life From a Dying Man

It was while I was in this unhappy condition— burdened, uptight, and continually driven to gain more and more of the things I believed would make me happy—that a call came from my mother early in the spring of 1973 with some shocking news: "Your cousin Dave has terminal cancer."

"No!" I thought. "Not Dave!" As young boys we were close cousins; the same age and good friends. Our families lived in neighboring towns and spent a lot of time together—visiting, sharing meals, and vacationing. Several times Dave and I rode our bicycles the 20 miles between our homes just to spend weekends together. As adults, however, our lives followed different paths, and at 32 he was early into his career as a minister.

I was dumbstruck by the news and my mind raced with questions. How could Dave be dying? The thought of death visiting someone as young as Dave—as young as me—had never entered my mind. Sure, I knew I could die at 85 or 90— anyone could. But death from cancer at 32? And why someone like Dave? Why now? What would happen to his wife and two young children? The questions whirled in my head, but no answers came.

As I tried to cope with the horrible news, my thoughts turned to what, if anything, I could do. I remembered Dave loved gospel music, so I phoned two of my associates and asked if they would go with me to the hospital in Santa Cruz, California, to sing some gospel songs.

The following Sunday morning we boarded a plane for San Jose. Flying was always an ordeal because—to put it bluntly—I was terrified the plane would crash and launch me into a less-than-certain eternal destiny. After boarding a plane, I would stare straight ahead, grip the arms of my seat until my knuckles turned white, and refuse to talk to anyone. Each time the plane bounced in the air currents I tensed up, afraid it would go down and I would wake up not in heaven, but in hell.

It wasn't that I hadn't professed to accept Christ in my youth. I had. I had even taught others how to be "saved by faith." But deep inside I was still uncertain where I stood before God. Was I really a Christian? In the final analysis would the way I lived my life have anything to do with where I ended up? I just didn't know for sure.

When we arrived at the hospital, my cousin and several patients were wheeled into a meeting room where we had arranged for a piano. Though Dave was completely coherent and chatted easily with us, I was shocked at his horribly sick condition. His spine was so fused by cancer he couldn't sit up, even in a wheelchair. Attendants rolled his bed into the room and positioned a mirror so he could see us as he lay flat on his back. His weight appeared to be down to 90 pounds or less, and I knew he was in terrible pain. He looked so frail—his face drawn, his color pale. His wife was sitting in a chair next to him, and his two small children stood there as well, barely able to reach his high hospital bed and hold his hand.

As I looked at Dave laying there so calmly with his family around him, a thought shook me like an earthquake:

That could be me! People do die young and unexpectedly—and I could be the man on that bed! I could be the one dying of cancer. I could be the one facing eternity within a matter of days.

Having never thought seriously about anyone dying, I was overcome by this dark specter of my own mortality. As I tried to cope with this new awareness of imminent death and eternity, panic overwhelmed me. I realized if I was the one dying, I could not say I had honestly lived even one day for the God I professed to know. In the face of death I was forced for the first time to acknowledge my true motives and priorities. On the outside my life may have appeared materially blessed, but on the inside I knew that I was spiritually impoverished.

As we sang several songs for Dave, he encouraged his wife and talked to his children. Even at this time of heaviness and sorrow his thoughts were not on himself—there was not a selfish thought in his heart.

As Dave listened, my friends sang a duet and I moved around and stood at the foot of his bed. Dave's face shone with a radiance I had never seen before. It was the way I imagined Stephen's face must have appeared as he stood before the council that condemned him to martyrdom.

> *At this point everyone in the Council chamber saw Stephen's face become as radiant as an angel's!*
> Acts 6:15 (TLB)

He was completely content, completely at peace, even in the face of death.

That's when another thought shook me with even greater force than before: *Dave has more peace in dying than I have in living!* What a horrible contrast! I stood there in my expensive suit—Dave's wasted body lay wrapped

7

in a cotton hospital gown. My jaw was set and my expression was grim—Dave's face wore a beautiful look of contentment. I was on my way to the world's assessment of financial success—Dave would never earn another penny. Soon I would return to my comfortable house and my waiting family—Dave would never again be at home with his loved ones.

In stark contrast to my life of pressure and an insatiable desire for more, I could see in Dave's countenance a serenity that was so appealing that I would have immediately given up everything in order to know that kind of peace. Then and there I was forced to admit to myself: Dave knew God in a way I didn't!

Though I had always thought of myself as a man who "knew about God," who kept all the rules, who tried to live like a Christian, I saw in Dave's life a relationship with God that I now desperately wanted to experience. I ached to know the Lord in the same way. But what was his secret? Where could I find his kind of peace? My belief had always been that God had "saved" me and given me eternal life, but it was up to me—at least in part—to arrange and control my circumstances in a way that would make me happy. When I did think about my relationship to the Lord, I usually viewed it as a partnership—I needed God to get me to heaven, but it was my duty to accomplish for myself most, if not all, of what I needed in this life.

But I could see that in spite of Dave's horrible condition—even life itself being completely out of his control—he possessed a peace which I had sought all my life and had never found. He had nothing and yet enjoyed perfect contentment; I had what I and the world considered "success" and was gulping down tranquilizers to cope with it.

How utterly ironic, I thought. Dave has everything I want—without having any of what I now have.

8

As I stood at the foot of his bed with my head down, I recalled several places in Scripture where God refers to Himself as the God of peace. I also thought of the peace and beauty of God's creation

> ## Dave has everything I want— without having any of what I have!

I had often observed in my travels and personal adventures. Then I remembered that one of Christ's personal titles is the Prince of Peace. I realized that the peace I longed for was far more than just the absence of trouble—it is the gift of God's peace and contentment, unchanging even in the midst of life's worst circumstances.

The Changing of the Gods

Finally, with my head still bowed, I made a decision I will never forget. I was so desperate to possess the inner peace I saw in Dave, I imagined unzipping my chest, reaching in with my right hand, taking hold of my heart, and handing it up to God. As I did, I earnestly and silently prayed:

"Lord, the life I've been living is too heavy and painful to live any more. I am desperate to know You and to experience the peace Dave has found in You. Please, Lord, take everything I am, everything I have, everything I value. Take my business, my title, whatever my success, my little material wealth. Take all the respect I've tried to gain. I want to trade it all in—just to know You."

Following my heart's desperate cry to be changed, I managed a last farewell to my beloved cousin, then followed as he was wheeled back to his room. Just before we left, Dave asked that we sing together "There's a Sweet, Sweet Spirit in This Place." When we finished singing, we silently filed out of his room and left for the airport.

Riding in the car, I thought about what had just happened. I knew my prayer of moments before was far different from any prayer I had ever prayed. Before, when challenged to commit my life to God, I only thought about trying to add "more God" to the other gods of my life—attempting to add more "religious" activity to my same old lifestyle.

> **A heart that is completely His is the key to freedom.**

However, it was at that moment standing by Dave's bed that I finally turned my back on all the things I had been driven to achieve and acquire, and longed with all my heart just to know God.

In time I would discover that this same *"heart that is completely His"* is the ongoing key to understanding and experiencing every freedom and spiritual benefit of the Christian life. As the Bible tells us in 2 Chronicles 16:9:

> *The eyes of the Lord move to and fro throughout the earth that He may strongly support those whose heart is completely His.*

On the flight home, I noticed something was distinctly different. I was no longer afraid to die! The tension was gone. I was at ease—even at 30,000 feet in the air. I sensed a peace and a freedom I had never known before.

> *I am leaving you with a gift—peace of mind and heart! And the peace I give isn't fragile like the peace the world gives. So don't be troubled or afraid.*
> John 14:27 (TLB)

Sometime later, Dave's father gave me a poem that conveyed in Dave's own words the real peace in pain I saw in him firsthand. This was the peace that I longed to know for myself, a peace God would begin to impart to my life over time as He patiently and graciously became Lord of my heart, mind, and will.

Make Me A Showcase

Lord, make my life a showcase
Of all Your power in me,
So that people watching cannot help but see
In my frail weakness, only You in me.

Make me worthy, Lord, to show it
The special peace You send in pain
Special strength for extra duties,
True humility in gain.

Make our home a showcase,
In each life You've gathered there,
Living out the love from Heaven,
With some left over, some to share.

Lord, let my life just be a showcase,
And I'll trust Your loving hand,
Whether in a high or low place,
Grace sufficient there to lend.

Freedom Can't Be Kept a Secret

People talk about a lot of things that, for the most part, are either the most exciting or most disturbing events of their lives. New grandparents, for example, can't help passing around pictures and bragging about their new grandchildren. The newly engaged woman bubbles over to just about everybody. And many who find themselves in some difficulty or challenge share that freely, too.

So why, for so many years, did it feel like such an effort to share my "Christian testimony"? Why didn't it just come naturally, and why did I think of "witnessing" only as my duty? Was it because my experience of "Christianity" didn't have the same joy as that of the newly engaged or the recent grandparent? Even more telling, was Jesus really not my Lord even though I said He was?

What I know today is that I have a new-found freedom that gives me such great joy—I can't keep it a secret!

—D.K.

2

Ride Share

Freedom in Christ Compels Me to Share

One thing I do know. I was blind but now I see!
John 9:25 (NIV)

That the generation to come might know, even the children yet to be born, That they may arise and tell them to their children, That they should put their confidence in God, And not forget the works of God, But keep His commandments.
Psalm 78:6-7

A Little More Background

Why I grew up feeling inferior I'm not totally sure, especially since my parents were the most loving any child could have. From my earliest childhood I can remember wanting them to be proud of me. Perhaps I felt a need to compete with my twin brother and younger sister for their approval and attention. Throughout my junior high and high school years, I longed to gain the acceptance of my peers—but I believed it constantly evaded me simply because I felt I wasn't very good at anything. I couldn't make first string in sports. My grades certainly didn't bring me any recognition. Although I had a car in my junior and senior years, I thought it was funny looking and not "cool." I was smaller in stature than the "buff" athletic types who were most popular on campus. Plus I felt marked as a "PK"—a preacher's kid—who was always considered odd and out-of-place because I didn't do the things everyone else did, or go the places they went.

All of this left me with an insatiable desire to excel at something, anything, in order to feel good about myself since I was not content with who I was. I began searching for something to fill the emptiness in my life, though I had no idea what that might be.

To try to make up for at least part of my feelings of inferiority, I began to lift weights—not just an occasional workout, but obsessively, no matter what else was on my schedule. Driven by my need, I exercised day after day on into my college years, adding bulk and size to my body. Even so, I left high school and entered college still craving something more.

In December of 1962, Sherryl and I married while we were still attending college. Out of necessity, I began looking for a way to make ends meet. I landed a job as a shoe salesman, but soon afterward a senior student from my hometown dropped by to tell me about his small building maintenance business. It had financed his way through college, and he wondered if I would be interested

> **I began searching for something to fill the emptiness in my life.**

in buying it. He had a few pieces of very used equipment, a rusted-out 1952 Chevrolet panel truck, and a total monthly income of $600. He was asking $2000 for the lot. I told him I didn't think I would be interested, but promised him that my wife and I would consider it. After some prayer, we began to think the little janitor business might be a good means of paying the bills until graduation. We agreed that if my dad would loan me the money, we would buy the company. He did, and soon we were in business—though we had never aspired to owning our own "company" (and certainly not doing janitorial work).

As we continued through college, our list of accounts grew because we ran our business the way we had been raised: with dedication and sincerity. We ended up with more buildings to clean than we could personally handle, so we hired several employees. Just the same, I thought of the company as nothing more than a stopgap, something just to get us through school.

Not long after graduating in 1965, however, I began to hear from several college friends whose early careers hadn't panned out. When they learned my company was still going, they asked if I would be interested in helping them get established in the same business in their hometowns. So over the next five years we launched five other small building maintenance companies, all with the same simple principles: honesty, quality, and dependability.

In 1970, my accountant recommended I see an attorney about incorporating to protect myself from personal liability. The lawyer, in turn, advised we structure our businesses as franchises, with the corporation as the franchisor. Most of what he said was well beyond my business knowledge; but when he informed me that I would take the title of "president," I sensed a rare feeling of fulfillment that I could only hope would counter my struggling self-image.

Through no ambition of our own—since I had never set out to start a business or to make our little enterprise something big—people started inquiring about our franchises: what they were, how much they sold for, where they were available, etc. Over the next three years we added 16 companies, which brought a surprise mixture of blessings and curses. On one hand, it felt good to be a business owner. On the other hand, I was still haunted by what I thought was everyone's perception of the building maintenance business. In addition, growth brought problems and pains that exposed me to fears, resentments, and anxieties I had never known.

> **I was driven by an unholy trinity —success, money, and respect.**

More business just seemed to bring more complaints— a substandard job, an employee that didn't even show up, a door left unlocked, restroom supplies not restocked by someone with something else on their mind. To me complaints were a fate worse than death. A customer with anger in his voice and a complaint on his lips meant I was losing: losing his confidence, losing a portion of my income, losing my credibility, possibly even losing my whole business—the one thing I felt I was becoming reasonably good at achieving.

So although my business was booming, the stress was steadily increasing. I continually felt compelled to grow, but at the same time feared I could lose it all. No matter what I personally achieved, nothing ever seemed to be enough. Fear of losing my one little success in life and my material security controlled me 24 hours a day.

Driven by an unholy trinity of success, money, and respect, I worked as hard as I could to reach some plateau in life that couldn't be threatened by people's disappointments and complaints. But it seemed no matter what I accomplished, my resentment and anger toward those who let me down only increased. In fact, every time the telephone rang, fear that it was another problem or complaint tightened the knot in my stomach. Finally, I was feeling so bad physically—constantly uptight and tense—I decided to see a doctor. He told me that if I didn't rid my life of some of the pressure, I would end up with an ulcer.

Because nothing seemed to remove the pain, I went back to the doctor two or three more times. On my third visit, he prescribed the tranquilizer Valium and told me to take them as often as I needed—but never more than three per day. Almost immediately I began taking up to six a day just to ease the stress that was continuing to build in my life. As I went for more refills the doctor warned me against "eating them like candy." But I was trapped in an endless spiral of pursuing what I thought was "success" and downing tranquilizers to cope with it.

> *What fools they are who manufacture idols for their gods. Their hopes remain unanswered.*
> Isaiah 44:9 (TLB)

Perhaps even worse than my experience of living with myself was everyone else's experience of having to live with me. Though I didn't understand how or why, my wife, friends, associates, and employees all seemed to fall short of my expectations.

When I walked into our home that my wife had carefully and laboriously worked to clean and decorate, I seemed to only notice that which wasn't perfect—a spot on the carpet, a crooked picture—any imperfection. At my office, work my staff did usually was evaluated on the basis of how it measured up to what I now know were unattainable standards. As a result, I nit-picked regularly.

Rather than looking for an opportunity to compliment the best in others, I was ready to tell them how they could and should do it better the next time.

All day every day, I felt I had to be in control—in control of what people thought of me, in control of my earthly destiny, and in control of my security. My entire being was consumed with control. No matter where my body was, my mind was usually far off in the distance analyzing, projecting, and anticipating upcoming events to make sure they were being ordered in the best possible way to maintain my success and be sensitive to anything that might threaten it.

> *Thus says the Lord, "**Cursed** [miserable] **is the man who trusts in mankind** and makes flesh his strength, and whose heart turns away from the Lord. For he will be like a bush in the desert and will not see when prosperity comes, but will live in stony wastes in the wilderness, a land of salt without inhabitant."*
> Jeremiah 17:5-6 (author's emphasis)

So it was in this insecure and internally tormented condition that I found myself—at the foot of my cousin's hospital bed—coming face-to-face with my desperate need for God. And though I certainly didn't foresee it at the time, that externally successful but internally disastrous life was the starting point for a journey of freedom and peace that continues to this day. It began when at the foot of my cousin's hospital bed, I gave Him my *whole* heart.

What God started that day has never ceased to amaze me as His peace has continued to invade areas of my life and circumstances I never dreamed possible.

My Pile of Stones

As the Lord began to liberate me from my fears,

inferiority, guilt, anger, jealousies, and stress, I felt compelled to keep a written record I could pass on to my children and grandchildren. I wanted something to serve as a testimony to future generations of my family, like the memorial of rocks the Israelites erected after God miraculously took them through the Jordan River to the land He had promised.

> *Let this be a sign among you, so that when your children ask later, saying, "What do these stones mean to you?" then you shall say to them, "Because the waters of the Jordan were cut off before the ark of the covenant of the Lord; when it crossed the Jordan, the waters of the Jordan were cut off." So these stones shall become a memorial to the sons of Israel forever.*
> Joshua 4:6-7

The more I thought about the memorial I wanted to leave to my children and grandchildren, the more I realized the message I longed to convey boiled down to five essential freedoms that form the foundation for this entire book. Like stones of a memorial, those five freedoms are:

Stone #1:
The world's success, excitement, and "fun" pale in comparison to the joy and fulfillment that comes from truly knowing the Lord.

Stone #2:
The "Christian life" is not a formula or something God expects us to do, but is the supernatural "heart surgery" He continues to perform as we earnestly seek to know Him.

21

Stone #3:

We cannot imagine how good God is. Anyone willing to trust Him with everything will live in awe of all He does.

Stone #4:

God is the essence of all that is practical. Whether it's something in the past, a problem today, or fear about tomorrow, believing exactly what God's Word says (no ifs, ands, or buts) brings clear direction and inner peace to every circumstance in life.

Stone #5:

My value and acceptability to God is based totally on what He has done for me, not on anything I could ever do for Him.

About 10 years ago I began jotting down notes and placing them in a manila folder in my desk. Several years later I asked an editor to help me compile them into some kind of an orderly manuscript. About halfway through that process he suggested I consider publishing the material.

> **The Christian life is not a formula.**

What began as a desk drawer file of notes for my kids has grown into this book.

In one sense I feel inadequate to communicate my story; but when I am asked or provided the opportunity, I usually begin by saying, *"I cannot begin to describe the freedom, the joy, the sense of eternal purpose, and the ever-increasing fulfillment God has brought into my life."* And I hasten to add that the marvel of my journey is that God is the One who has continued to produce these freedoms as the result of only one continuing decision on my part: to know and experience Him more than anything else.

So my purpose in writing is not to give examples of lifestyle changes that a reader should try to work on to improve family or business relations. Rather, it is to praise and honor God for all He's done for me, with a prayer that many others will desire to seek the Lord as their number one priority.

For the reader who may wonder whether I was actually a Christian before my cousin's death, I can only answer, "I don't know." What I do know today is that I identify with the joy of the man liberated from demon possession in Mark 5. He was so thrilled with the freedom the Lord had given him that he wanted to stay with Jesus. The Lord, however, turned to him and said:

> *Go home to your people and report to them what great things the Lord has done for you, and how He had mercy on you.*
> Mark 5:19

Make no mistake: my external world is not much different than it was before my cousin's death. In some ways, life in general offers more difficulties and challenges now than it did then. The task of running a business is as much a minefield of problems, crises, and complaints as it ever was.

The wonderful joys I write and speak about are not the result of changes in my circumstances. The real differences are not external and material; they are *internal* and *spiritual*. They are the result of the things that God, in His mercy, has done for me over the past 20 years. And they are the way that God can take *anyone*, even Daryl Kraft, and continue to transform their lives so that every day they experience a little more of His peace and freedom.

Do you want more and more of God's kindness and peace? Then learn to know him better and better.

2 Peter 1:2 (TLB)

But the path of the righteous is like the light of dawn, that shines brighter and brighter until the full day.

Proverbs 4:18

Stress   Joy

(All Self-Effort)   (All Heart Condition)

Stress (All Self-Effort)	Joy (All Heart Condition)
• *Trying to be a better Christian*	• *Desiring to better know the Lord (2 Peter 1:2)*
• *Participating faithfully in my church*	• *My life's greatest passion is to know God (Proverbs 2:1-10)*
• *Reading the Bible because I should*	• *Reading the Bible because I hunger for spiritual food (1 Peter 2:2-5)*
• *Trying to obey the "do's and don'ts" of Christianity*	• *Wanting to be totally changed, filled, and led by the Lord (Psalm 51:10-13)*
• *Wanting to serve the Lord*	• *Wanting to become more like the Lord (Ephesians 5:1)*
• *Memorizing verses*	• *Meditating on Scripture verses (Joshua 1:8)*
• *Desiring to work for God*	• *Desiring God to work in me (Psalms 139:23-24)*
• *Witnessing*	• *Sharing (Mark 5:19)*
• *Decision: Repeated rededication*	• *Decision: Desiring the death of "me" in my life (Galatians 2:20)*

—D.K.

3

Choose the Course

Freedom to Pursue a New Passion

"If you seek her as silver, and search for her as for hidden treasures . . . ."

Proverbs 2:4

Those moments at Dave's bedside will be forever etched in my memory as the "memorial" where my journey of freedom began. Although I didn't fully understand what happened or even how to talk about it, I did know—with absolute certainty—that now I had a growing desire to know God in a way far greater than I had ever known before.

The next evening at home, I gathered my Bible and several study books to begin preparing a new series of Sunday school lessons for my class. (Remember, I was already deeply involved in church activities out of a sense of duty.) Our previous series on Revelation was coming to a close, so I had asked the class to choose another book of the Bible. I offered either Romans or Genesis, since I already had outlines and commentaries from my college courses (which I figured would save a lot of preparation time). But the class ignored my suggestions and insisted on the book of Proverbs. That was unfamiliar territory; but eventually I agreed to make it our study for the next year.

So, armed with a new-found curiosity, that night after dinner I read the first two chapters of Proverbs in *The Living Bible*. Several verses immediately caught my eye:

> *"These are the proverbs of King Solomon of Israel, David's son . . . "* (1:1).

> *"He wrote them to teach his people how to live—how to act in every circumstance . . . "* (1:2).

> *". . . for wisdom and truth will enter the very center of your being, filling your life with joy"* (2:10).

I read the verses again, then slowly for a third time with growing amazement. They seemed to describe exactly what I had witnessed and so desperately desired just the day before when I was with my cousin. I was particularly drawn to the phrase "filling your life with joy."

No sooner had I re-read those words than I began to wonder what exactly a person would have to do to experience a "life *filled* with joy." I went back and re-read Proverbs 2:1-5:

> *"My son, if you will receive my sayings, and treasure my commandments within you, make your ear*

attentive to wisdom, incline your heart to understanding; for if you cry for discernment, lift your voice for understanding; if you seek her as silver, and search for her as for hidden treasures; then you will discern the fear of the Lord, and discover the knowledge of God."

Proverbs 2:1-5

Notice that one word is repeated several times in this passage: "*if.*" In fact, Solomon used it three times in five verses! Even more significant, he used it three times in one long sentence. Solomon seemed intent on underscoring one primary thought. Read the passage one more time and insert your name within the brackets, and begin, as I did, to hear a paraphrase of what this Scripture seems to be saying: "[Daryl] *if* you will . . . then your life will be filled with wisdom and joy. [Daryl] once again, *if* you will . . . then your life will be filled with joy. [Daryl] you still don't seem to understand. Let me repeat it one more time. [Daryl] only *if* you will . . . *then* you will begin to experience God's wisdom and joy."

My curiosity was intense. Although I was already beginning to experience a new peace, I didn't clearly understand why. I realized that these verses gave conditions that had to be met if I was to discover and experience a brand new life "filled with joy." At that moment I was so consumed with the desire for understanding, that nothing could have distracted me. Let's read the passage one more time:

"If . . . if . . . if . . . you search for her as you would for lost hidden treasure . . . ."

That's it!

29

God is telling us that His insight and discernment which results in a "life filled with joy" is available to those who earnestly search for them as they would for a lost, hidden treasure. But what does that mean?

The Search for Lost Treasure

I remember a time early in our marriage when Sherryl lost the diamond from her engagement ring. The thought of losing one of our few material assets

> **When I want to find God more than anything else—I will.**

threw me into a panic. She believed it had fallen somewhere in the carpet of our home, so during the next week I crawled for hours each evening on my hands and knees, searching every square inch until my fingers were red and sore. Even when I left home for the office, I continued the search in my mind, desperately trying to figure out where that small, hidden treasure could be.

Now, in the present, I wondered what lost earthly treasure would create such a deep desperation that the search for it would become my number one passion. I quickly eliminated material possessions: car, house, furnishings—they didn't seem that important anymore. Instead, I found myself considering the panic I would feel if my wife suddenly vanished.

I imagined the anguish I would feel if I came home from work one evening expecting to see Sherryl—but instead, found she had mysteriously disappeared. *Her car's here, but she's not. Six o'clock and she's not home for dinner. She's always here or calls to let me know she'll be late—what's wrong? Seven o'clock, and still no call, no message, no clue. Eight o'clock!* I begin frantically calling all our friends. *They haven't seen her. No one has. And still no word from her.* I call the authorities to alert them as my anxiety grows. *Nine o'clock!* Panic is beginning to paralyze me. *Ten o'clock!* I'm an emotional cripple, imagining the worst. *I may never see her again!* Desperation increases as I exhaust all possibilities. *Where is my wife? Where is my wife? Where is she?*

I recognized that regardless of anything else I might "need" to do, my consuming desire would be to find Sherryl. Though life would go on—eating, sleeping, working—the prevailing passion of my innermost being would be to find my wife.

As I began to understand the incredible urgency that would overwhelm everything else as I desperately sought to find my wife, I realized this was the same depth of intensity I felt just the day before—to find and know God. I was astonished to realize that never before—not once in the previous 32 years—had I ever felt that kind of intense desire to really know God. Further, it began to dawn on me that this was undoubtedly the reason why, even while believing I was "serving God" with all my religious activities, I had no peace and was miserable for so many years.

> **God's peace comes from knowing Him —not from doing things for Him.**

As a preacher's kid, I tried to walk the tightrope of "Christian" rules—primarily out of respect for my loving and godly parents. I grew up watching them give comfort to others with little regard to any personal convenience, and never saw anything I considered un-Christlike. So, not wanting to embarrass them and not understanding the difference between rules and the relationship with Christ my parents enjoyed, I never drank a drop of alcohol or tried smoking. I never swore, gambled, or engaged in sex before marriage—and, of course, I faithfully attended church. Because I abstained from "bad" things and did some good things, I considered myself a "good" Christian.

However, following the "rules" of Christianity was entirely different from what I was now beginning to understand. God's peace and joy for our lives comes from a consuming passion to know Him, not merely from doing things for Him. Up to this time in my life I read and studied the Bible primarily to memorize verses, to pass a test in school, to debate with those of different religions, or to teach a class.

Often, out of a sense of duty, I tried to "have my devotions," but I didn't enjoy it most of the time and seldom remembered what I read. Sometimes I would even fall asleep soon after starting. Now I found myself studying with a brand new passion simply to *know* God.

Knowing God

What does it mean to know God? In a very real sense it means the same thing as getting to know a neighbor, a friend, a fiancee, or anyone. When we desire to get to know someone and find out what they are really like, we talk to them, we listen to them, we develop an interest in what interests them, and we value their ideas and input into our lives. The best way to do all that in a relationship with God is by spending time in His Word—the Bible.

But someone may ask, "How can I discipline myself to study God's Word?" Do we have to "discipline" ourselves to do what we really enjoy? For example, do people who have a passion for baseball, history, romance, or adventure, have to force themselves to read books about it? Does a Dodger fan have to force himself to go to a game? Does a vacationing couple have to force themselves to go to Hawaii?

A passion to study God's Word is not aroused by rigid self-discipline. The "discipline" to study God's Word arises from a passion to know Him. God Himself imparts to us a deep love for His Word when we lay down all our other "loves" and make knowing Him our greatest priority. This isn't work

—it's a heartfelt desire. It isn't ritual — it's a relationship that grows in joy and meaning with every new discovery.

Almost from the first moment I began to desire God's control over my heart, mind, and will, many verses I quoted from memory for years started to come alive and deeply convict my heart of wrongs I had not seen previously. Gradually, as I accepted each new light from God's Word, He began to change what I believed, what I valued, how I thought, how I acted, how I lived, how I viewed others, and how I felt inside. There was also a growing hunger within me to read the Bible at every opportunity, always with the prayer, "Lord, I just want to know *You* better."

One of the first evident changes was the disappearance of my constant need for tranquilizers—and it never returned. I also noticed I had stopped biting my fingernails; in fact, they were beginning to grow. To some, this may not seem like much of a miracle, but for 32 years my mother, and then my wife, tried without success to help break my compulsive habit. Now my fingernails were growing and I wasn't even trying to keep from biting them. To me, having normal fingernails for the past 20 years is indeed a true miracle, a significant outward evidence that God has given me the inner peace He promised.

As the Lord begins to reshape your life, you will find, as I did, that studying His Word is like tasting candy. Each new insight produces an even greater desire to know more of Him and His righteousness—and in turn, another new freedom. Because it "tastes so good," you want to go back for more.

"Those who love Thy law have great peace . . ."
Psalm 119:165

33

> *"When your words came, I ate them; they were my joy and my heart's delight."*
> Jeremiah 15:16 (NIV)

It's Not Where I Am,
It's Who I Am

Too often in trying to discover or understand God's will for my life, I've been more concerned with where I should be than who I should be. And quite honestly, dealing with the where was never as convicting as dealing today with the who. Maybe that's why in past years I usually chose to associate "God's will" with a place and not a "be-ing."

God's Word places a far greater emphasis on who I am than on where I am. For example, Paul said to the Ephesians:

"*. . . put off your old self. . .*" (4:22 - NIV);

"*. . . and to put on the new self. . .*" [right where we are currently living] (4:24);

"*Serve wholeheartedly, as if you were serving the Lord, not men,*" [wherever we are, whatever we are doing] (6:7 - NIV).

And to the Colossians:

"*. . .be filled with the knowledge of His will. . .*" (1:9 - NASB);

"so that you may walk [wherever you are] *in a manner worthy of the Lord, to please Him in all respects, bearing fruit in every good work . . . "* [leaving a witness for Christ where we are] (1:10).

So is the hypocrisy that the world sees in Christians primarily due to our being in the wrong place, or the wrong they see in our "being" where we are?

—D.K.

4

Wrong Way

Freedom from the Myth of Greener Grass

"Usually a person should keep on with the work
he was doing when God called him."
1 Corinthians 7:20 (TLB)

As I continued to experience the new freedoms, I assumed God would move me away from the harrowing "dog eat dog" world of business that brought so much stress into my personal and family life. I thought He would direct me into "full-time Christian service." But *I* had no idea how to make such a move.

"Full-time" Where I Am

Because of his many years in the ministry, my dad was a natural source of advice. So I called and arranged for us to meet in the study of his church in Los Altos. As soon as I arrived I shared my recent spiritual experience and my newfound desire to know and live for the Lord. I assumed that truly serving God would mean selling the business I hated, enrolling in seminary, and setting out like the disciples to live on whatever income people gave me to support my family and ministry.

After I presented what I considered my options—the pastorate, the mission field, evangelistic work—Dad's answer surprised me: "You don't necessarily need to do any of those things. God first wants you to live for Him right where you are. Then if He wants to move you, He will move you."

I thought, "What kind of an answer is that? I just spent hard-earned money for an airplane ticket and lost a day's work just to hear my dad tell me to go back home and keep doing what I hate—only now do it for God?"

> **"How would the Lord do what I'm doing right now?"**

Because I loved and respected my father so much, I didn't reject his counsel; but it left me totally confused. I left his office without the foggiest idea how to understand what he told me. Viewing my career as a ministry was an option I had never even considered.

In the coming weeks, his words, "live for God right where you are," continued to challenge me as I went about my day-to-day activities. I began to ask myself how the Lord would respond to each complaint, each criticism, each comment. How would He make each company policy; arrive at a decision to hire; daily encourage, correct, or discharge employees? How would He make plans for the future? At each point the thought that continued to echo in my head was, "How would the Lord do what I am doing right now?"

As I continued to think about my dad's advice, God brought to mind the "ifs" I had read in the second chapter of Proverbs. I turned again to that portion of His Word, and the Lord opened my eyes to another new insight. In the verse following the "ifs" of Proverbs 2:1-4 was the word "then."

> ". . . *then wisdom will be given you . . .*"
> Proverbs 2:4 (TLB)

Solomon didn't say *if* our greatest passion is to know God *then* we will discover His will sometime in the future. Rather, he said that if we *really* desire to know Him, God's will and purpose will become operative in our lives.

Notice also that God did not say *if* we long to know Him we would need to suddenly change our *career* (or circumstances) in order to serve Him. Instead, He said that He will begin to change our *character* in a way that glorifies Him *right where we are.*

> "*Then you will discern righteousness* [character change] . . . *justice* [character change] . . . *equity* [character change]. "
> Proverbs 2:9

It's as if the Lord is saying, "I'm calling you to stay where you are and to hunger and thirst after me in the midst of the very problems you believed made you miserable.

I'm calling you first to a heart change, not to a 'place' change."

God calls all Christians to full-time Christian *lives*— some in the pulpit, some on foreign mission fields, some in secular careers. In every situation, His purpose is to transform His adopted children so that others *in all walks of life* can see His righteousness in them. This is precisely what our Lord was teaching in Matthew 5:16:

> *"Let your light* [new character] *shine before men* [where you live and work] *in such a way [different from the character of the rest of the world] that they may see your good works* [Christlikeness] *and glorify your father who is in heaven."*
>
> Matthew 5:16

As God allowed me to begin understanding this wonderful liberty, I wrote down one of the greatest freedoms I've ever discovered: If God's will is my number one priority, I'm already in it! "If . . . if . . . if . . ," *then* He is at work in my life!

Today, some Christians still talk about struggling to "find the will of God." They wonder and worry constantly where it is, whether they are in it, or if not, how they can find it. The answer is to believe in God's sovereignty—in His absolute control of all things—and then place your confidence in the fact that desiring Him to change your heart, right where you are, is His perfect will for you.

Anytime our hearts cry out, "I wish I weren't here," it is a type of silent, deceived rebellion against God. On the other hand, our willingness to face even the most adverse

> **If God's will is my number one priority— I'm in it!**

and unpleasant circumstances in submission to Him affirms our confidence that He ultimately is in control of all things.

During my stress-filled years, I focused more on changing my circumstances than allowing God to change my attitude and character. When I was unhappy with school, I thought only about quitting. When I didn't like church, I considered moving our membership. When I didn't like my work, I looked for a new career.

> **Discouragement is never God's method of direction —it is always Satan's diversion.**

But once I understood that God's will has to do first with who I am instead of where I am, I began asking God to change me instead of asking Him to change my circumstances.

God's Word tells us:

> *"Blessed is the man who trusts in the Lord and whose trust is the Lord. For he will be like a tree planted by the water* [wherever he is], *that extends its roots by a stream and will not fear* [get discouraged] *when the heat comes; but its leaves will be green, and it will not be anxious* [stressful] *in a year of drought nor cease to yield its fruit."*
>
> Jeremiah 17:7-8

It appears, then, that God wants to keep our "leaves" green *through* heat and drought, instead of moving us to a place of less heat and drought. Discouragement is never God's method of direction—it is Satan's diversion from God's perfect will in our lives. This doesn't mean God won't allow difficult circumstances into our experiences; it only means He provides us with the option of focusing on Him and His perfect, loving control rather than on our difficulties.

Recently, a woman whose husband had just left her called to ask my opinion on an incidental matter. While we were visiting, I asked her how her relationship with the Lord was going. Seven months earlier, my wife and I encouraged her to commit her problems, including her troubled marriage, to the Lord. At that time she had said, "I'm afraid to. I'm really afraid of what He might want me to do."

Now she shared a new and different outlook: "I can't begin to tell you how much peace and joy God has given since I began to trust Him and pray. Even though my husband has left, even though my children and I are living with my in-laws because I don't have enough money to rent a place of my own, God has given me a wonderful peace. I wouldn't trade it for anything in the world."

Obviously, her outward circumstances had not improved. If anything, they had grown worse. Yet she had discovered that God was able to meet her deepest inward needs *right where she was*.

First Church of the Janitors

My twin brother, Gerry, is involved in a church-planting and evangelism ministry in Canada. Not long ago he asked us to open our home to one of his friends who was in the U.S. seeking financial support for his ministry.

As we visited after dinner, we discussed his work. I learned of many formidable problems facing his ministry: churches with congregations too small to pay their overhead and a minister's salary; ministers discouraged by a lack of response; dissension over theological viewpoints; moral lapses of some leaders.

Finally our conversation turned to what I did for a living. As I told my brother's friend about our business, he listened politely and then asked, "Daryl, have you ever thought about going into full-time Christian service?" I'm not sure what he was thinking. Perhaps he assumed that most of a businessman's life is focused only on making money when it could be spent saving souls. Or maybe he simply sensed the desire God has given me to serve Him. Either way, I knew his question was well-intended.

So the following morning I took my guest on a tour of our offices. I shared how God had changed my purpose in life, transformed my attitude toward people, and reshaped the focus of our entire company. He saw how we maintain regular communication with franchises, our many publications, and the regular conferences to encourage managers in their personal and professional lives. I shared our tape ministry, our support services, and our executive leadership and marriage and family seminars. I also told him about our unique group of franchisees, and how many of them desire that God use their lives and businesses for His glory.

Finally he said, "Daryl, I want to learn how you do all this. It almost looks like you have 70 'churches' you provide with regular encouragement and support."

Believers today have a tremendous opportunity to dispel the myth of the greener grass. We should encourage Christians to allow God's character to shine through them *right where they are* by permitting God, through His Word and the power of His Spirit, to change their character. As employers we have the unusual opportunity to demonstrate God's love to those employees who do not know Him personally or ever visit a church where they can hear what God has to offer them.

The first great opportunity for Christians in business is to *show* the life and peace God has brought to their marriages and families. Then, when given the opportunity, they can share the eternal purpose, joy, and freedom only He can give.

For many years I imagined my life divided into compartments, much like slices of a pie. I viewed "serving the Lord" (which to me meant being involved in religious activity several hours each week) as one important slice, with family, career, recreation, and other priorities making up the rest of the pie. Though I did not consciously try to exclude God, anytime I was involved in business, family, or other issues, I never thought these related to "full-time Christian service" because they obviously were not religious activities.

God's Word, however, seems to indicate that true "full-time" ministry is allowing Him to show the difference He makes in our character all the time—in *all* our relationships. He wants everyone we come into contact with to *see* the difference He makes in our attitudes, morality, honesty, and every other area—rather than just hearing the words of an occasional testimony or devotional from one "slice" of our lives.

As I continue in business today, someone occasionally brings up my old perspective of the "full-time service" greener grass. What freedom there is in recognizing that while the Lord has specifically directed many into ministry-related vocations, He also gives the rest of us, as His children, unlimited ministry opportunities in all our careers. For all of us, His "full-time" service is *at hand.*

It begins with "full-time Christian character" right where we are.

"... *that you may prove yourselves to be blameless and innocent, children of God above reproach **in the midst of a crooked and perverse generation**, among whom you appear as lights in the world* . . . ."
Philippians 2:15

God is Good

Before my experience at Dave's bedside, God seemed relevant primarily to my eternal destiny. Since then, however, the Lord has become light for everything in my life.

• The more I grow in understanding God's true character—that He is totally sovereign and totally good—the more I'm drawn to commit my anxiety to Him instead of trying harder on my own.

• The more I grow in knowing Him—His unconditional love, His compassion, His purpose—the more I desire to be like Him.

• The more I grow in understanding the completeness of His grace toward me, the more I want Him to live through me because I'm free, instead of feeling I need to try harder in a false hope of becoming "free."

• The more I understand of Him, the more I realize He's the answer to any and every problem I might ever encounter.

—D.K.

5

The Obstacle Course

Freedom from Doubts about God's Goodness

*"The Lord is **always good**. He is always loving and kind, and His faithfulness goes on and on to each succeeding generation."*

Psalm 100:5 (TLB)

Prior to Dave's death, I had somehow convinced myself that a total personal commitment to Jesus Christ as Lord of my life would mean giving up nearly everything—if not everything—I hoped to enjoy. When a speaker or pastor in my church issued a call to total surrender to Christ, I was always hesitant because I feared that if I stood in agreement, I would lose much of the freedom to pursue those things I believed would bring greatest happiness. As silly as it sounds now, I was most fearful that God might ask me to go as a missionary to some remote part of the earth where I would be forced to endure a life of hardship and then die of some dreaded disease.

Heaven Has Fishing Holes?

If someone had actually put me on the spot back then and asked me whether I would rather go to heaven or hell, I would (of course) have quickly replied, "Heaven." But if that same person would have given me a third option, that of staying right here on earth, I would have admitted, "I would prefer to stay here – providing I can build a secure fence around my family and continue to enjoy the things I enjoy." Some of my greatest experiences in life revolved around outdoor pursuits—riding mules into the rugged backcountry of the American southwest, tracking calf-killing predators, camping, and fishing the streams and ocean waters of the far northern Pacific.

> **I could only relate to heaven in terms I understood, like "streets of gold."**

In my heart, I couldn't imagine how any experience in heaven could measure up to the fun times and fishing holes I experienced here on earth.

Granted, I knew the Bible talked about things like "streets of gold"—but how much fun could they be compared to catching a 40-pound salmon?

Some time after I started on my journey of freedom, however, I began to realize that my attitude must be wrong. It was the same as saying, "God isn't all *that* good. Sure, He saved me from an eternity in hell, and I'm grateful for that; but if the eternal kingdom doesn't offer my kind of outdoor thrills, how can I possibly look forward to being there—bored forever!"

Back then, those were my honest feelings. In those days I really didn't know God in a close and personal way. So, given a choice, I would rather spend eternity with the fun and fishing holes I knew than spend it with an impersonal God I respected only from a distance. Furthermore, as long as material things were what I desired and valued most, I could only relate to heaven in terms I understood, like "streets of gold."

Satan had so blinded my eyes that I was worshipping the material world God had created instead of the God who created it—I favored the creation over the Creator. I accepted the "fun" and "excitement" of those excursions as a cheap counterfeit of God's priceless joy, blessing, and fulfillment.

I still enjoy some outdoor activities, but I'm continuing to see that they pale in comparison to the ever-increasing reality of spending eternity with the One who has become so meaningful to me.

Through consistent study of God's Word, I am growing to understand Him in a way that far exceeds any material dimension. In fact, I think I'm just beginning to understand what Paul wrote to the church at Corinth:

> *"No eye has seen, no ear has heard, no mind has conceived what God has prepared for those who love Him."*
>
> 1 Corinthians 2:9 (NIV)

Realizing that heaven's goodness is still so far beyond what the Lord has come to mean to me, I can only respond with gratitude and joy.

People vary widely in their tastes for things they enjoy. For some, fishing, hiking, hunting, and all that is included in "the great outdoors" holds no attraction. Some people are more stimulated by computers with lightning speed; or

51

traveling to faraway places; or sampling the finest cuisine; or shopping; or enjoying the security of a lifelong friendship; or any of a host of other earthly experiences.

Yet this verse indicates that it is impossible for any of us to fully conceive of that which God has prepared for those who love Him. Even the total fulfillment of our wildest dreams, fantasies, and life's most meaningful experiences will fall far short of the reality our eternal future holds.

Tour of Heaven

Not long ago I was discussing with a friend my growing relationship with the Lord and how it was dramatically changing my view of heaven. I shared how I now look forward to being there some day, and how my perspective had completely changed on the passing of a loved one or friend.

As I continued sharing, however, I noticed a growing sense of anguish in my friend's face. Finally she confided, "Daryl, if my daughter were to die, I don't think I could ever be happy!"

I knew exactly how she felt. Many times I have feared the unthinkable—how sad and lonely my own life would be if God ever chose to take a loved one. I said to her, "I realize how deep a love God has placed in our hearts for our loved ones, friends, family . . . and I would never minimize the human loss and sorrow we would feel if death were to invade those precious relationships."

I went on, however, to ask her to imagine that God suddenly appeared before us, introduced Himself to both of us, and asked if I would mind if He took her on a quick tour of heaven. I then asked her to further imagine that He whisked her off to the heavenly realm. There she saw the Lord face to face and experienced what it would actually be like to live forever where there is no sin, no sorrow, no pain, no injustice—only eternal joy in the presence of a God who loves us unconditionally.

"Now," I continued, "you've just returned, and you're talking to me. Tell me how you think you'd feel about your daughter going there someday. Even knowing how much you would miss her, would you be happier for her if she had to live here longer, or happier if she got to go there sooner?" As we continued to talk about our hope of heaven, and the thought of spending eternity with the One who has brought such complete meaning and fulfillment to our lives, my friend's countenance began to change from one of fear to one of assurance.

God is the supreme "Good," and what we perceive to be "good," "enjoyable," or "fun" in this fallen, decaying world is but a pale shadow of the infinite goodness and joy we will experience with Him in His eternal kingdom.

Only the Knives

An encounter many years ago with my youngest son shed new light on the perfect goodness of God, and how He deals with us only out of His infinite goodness.

One evening, my wife and I walked into our kitchen, and saw, to our horror, that our little three-year-old boy was standing across the room with a razor-sharp butcher knife in each hand. He had found them in a kitchen drawer, and now they were his two favorite toys. He clanged them together and flashed them back and forth in front of his face. Of course, we knew we had to get the knives away from him, but we had to figure out how to do so without frightening him, or worse yet, leading him to think we were playing a game of "chase."

Finally, by moving very slowly and pretending not to notice him, we were able to get close enough that I could grab both his hands and hold him while Sherryl took the knives. As expected, he sceamed and cried in protest as we "deprived" him of his treasures, totally unaware of how close he had come to seriously hurting or possibly fatally injuring himself.

It is time we gained a new understanding of the goodness of God's Word and what our obedience to Him really means. *From His perfect eternal perspective, God never wants to take the truly good things from our lives— only the "knives."* Total submission to the Lord never eliminates any true joy or fulfillment, only the painful consequences of sin.

> *"'For I know the plans that I have for you,' declares the Lord, 'plans for welfare and not for calamity to give you a future and a hope.'"*
> Jeremiah 29:11

God Gets "Gooder"

Further, in terms of God's goodness, when life beyond our control seems to have dealt us all a bad hand, God gives us His great assurance:

> *"And we know that God* [ultimately] *causes all things to* **work together for good** *to those who love God, to those who are called according to His purpose."*
> Romans 8:28

Yes, the Bible declares our loving Heavenly Father is at work bringing "good" out of "all things." Everywhere we turn in Scripture, in fact, we discover more and more of God's goodness. Psalm 119:97-105 reads:

"O how I love Thy law!
It is my meditation all the day.
Thy commandments make me wiser than my enemies,
For they are ever mine.
I have more insight than all my teachers,
For Thy testimonies are my meditation.
I understand more than the aged,
Because I have observed Thy precepts.
I have restrained my feet from every evil way,
That I might keep Thy word.
I have not turned aside from Thine ordinances,
For Thou Thyself hast taught me.
How sweet are Thy words to my taste!
Yes, sweeter than honey to my mouth!
From Thy precepts I get understanding;
Therefore I hate every false way.
Thy word is a lamp to my feet,
And a light to my path."

I often begin my Sunday school lessons with the statement: "This past week I found God to be even 'gooder' than I've ever understood before." Of course there's no such word—but I feel the words don't exist to adequately describe God's goodness toward each one of us. We need only to have a passion to know Him and He will continue to reveal more of Himself— His *unconditional* love, His *complete* forgiveness, His *total* compassion, His *amazing* grace, His *daily* guidance, and His *eternal* security. That is how He desires to reveal Himself to all His children. As James 1:17 tells us:

"Every good thing bestowed and every perfect gift is from above, coming down from the Father of lights, with whom there is no variation, or shifting shadow."

And, as the Psalmist stated so eloquently in Psalm 107:9:

> *"He has satisfied the thirsty soul, and the hungry soul He has filled **with what is good.**"*

Anxious For Nothing

Even after my cousin's death and its immediate effect in my life, my greatest anxiety for years was that I would still somehow fail to live for the Lord as consistently as I felt He wanted me to. What if I couldn't be a "good enough" Christian? And, even a more torturous thought, what if my children never made a real commitment of their hearts to God?

One day, however, God opened my eyes to verses I had read many times—had even memorized—but had never experienced:

> *"**Be anxious for nothing,** but in everything by prayer and supplication with thanksgiving let your requests be made known to God. And the peace of God, which surpasses all comprehension, shall guard your hearts and your minds in Christ Jesus."*
>
> Philippians 4:6-7

As I re-read these verses, I began to understand that God was offering freedom from two of the biggest worries in my life: worry about my own spiritual growth, and worry about my children's commitment to Christ. In fact, the longer

> **The Bible is about the Master Surgeon and what He does as we leave our whole heart in His hands.**

I looked, the more I realized the word *nothing* included anything and everything I might be anxious about.

Once I submitted myself before God in my heart, I realized that worry is actually a sin, and I began to believe what God had said all along. And as I committed to Him *whatever* I was worried about, I realized with tears of joy that I could entrust even my kids to Him, instead of living under the weight of thinking I needed to "fix" them myself. The freedom from worry Christ gives each one of us is as though He is telling us, "You can't accomplish anything for me in your own life or your kids' lives. All you can do is admit to me you can't, and then let me accomplish my purpose in and through you."

Don't read the Bible in terms of what you should "do" or "work on" to improve in your life, but in terms of all that the Master Surgeon will do as you continue to leave your whole heart in His hands. This is what Paul was emphasizing to the Philippians when he wrote:

> *" . . . He* [God] *who began a good work in you will perfect it until the day of Christ Jesus."*
>
> Philippians 1:6

He did *not* say, "He who began a good work in you now expects *you* to perfect it!"

One of Our Jordan Rivers

In the book of Joshua we see practical applications of God's goodness in everyday living as the hand of a loving God leads His people on to greater, not lesser, joys and blessings.

Early in the book we find an official account of the way God fulfilled His promise to Abraham by giving His people the land of Canaan, a land "flowing with milk and honey," a land much better than the wilderness where they had wandered for 40 years. This account reveals that *God always leads us to something better when our hearts are completely His.* That is not to say that God will not allow our faith to be challenged, our health to be threatened, or our heart to be broken in order to help us grow spiritually. But that which He has for us is far better than anything we can provide for ourselves.

For example, God told Joshua to do something that appeared totally impossible—cross the Jordan River. A fording at flood stage would have involved as much as a mile and a half of treacherous river. But God's command to believe Him for the seemingly impossible did not nullify His goodness. He simply performed a miracle and dried up the portion of the river in front of them. This not only allowed the children of Israel to cross safely, it provided them with a lifelong memorial to God's miraculous ability to do for them what they could not do for themselves.

Thinking back, there have been times in our family when difficulties with our children have seemed as insurmountable as crossing the raging Jordan. We struggled with problems that ranged from an apparent lack of interest in spiritual things and an attraction to worldly things, to a temper so uncontrollable that at times we wondered if we were witnessing demon possession.

Finally we were brought to our knees by a realization of how completely and utterly helpless we were to change our children. We had done everything we knew how to do, and we hadn't seen even a glimmer of hope. Then, from a point of total helplessness, we finally understood that God wanted us to believe that He was "good" enough to be trusted even with the eternal destinies of our children.

It was amazing. As we began to trust Him instead of ourselves, He began replacing our worry and fear with peace. This in turn made a noticeable and growing difference in our attitudes. We found we no longer argued with our kids out of a feeling we must change them. Instead, we began to calmly give them advice from God's Word, and then commit the situation to the Lord. As a result of the changes God was making first in our lives as parents, we continued to see gradual changes—to His glory—in the lives of our kids.

> **Believing what God says = freedom.**

Like the children of Israel at the banks of the Jordan, we see God—in His time, not ours—doing what we are totally unable to do in our own strength. This does not mean everything with our kids is always the way we would choose. But to this day, continually going to our knees and giving the Lord every worry and anxiety about our children still brings us peace and freedom in our relationships with them.

The Search to Know God

In a continuing search to know God, at least three great aspects of His character have become increasingly real, freeing me to remain positive and confident in *whatever* negative and uncertain times:

• *God is good.*

David began Psalm 92 with the statement, *"It is good to say 'Thank you' to the Lord...,"* then ended the chapter by saying it is because *"He is my shelter. There is **nothing but goodness in Him"** (TLB)

Psalm 34:10 echoes this thought with the statement:

> *"They who seek the Lord shall not be in want of any good thing."*

Real freedom in Christ begins when we understand and believe that everything God gives and everything God allows in our lives is filtered through His perfect and absolute goodness—no matter how things *appear* to us at the time.

• *God is in control.*

David wrote:

> *"Yours is the mighty power and glory and victory and majesty. Everything in the heavens and earth is yours, O Lord, and this is your kingdom. We adore you as being **in control of everything**."*
>
> 1 Chronicles 29:11 (TLB)

In Proverbs, Solomon said:

> *"**Since the Lord is directing** our steps, why try to understand everything that happens along the way?"*
>
> Proverbs 20:24 (TLB)

In Job, we read:

> *"I know that **You can do everything**, and that no purpose of Yours can be withheld from You."*
>
> Job 42:2 (NKJV)

God frees our hearts, our thoughts, and our attitudes as we accept without question that He is always in control of everything that affects our lives. Nothing ever "falls through the cracks." He is in absolute control.

• *God works all things together for good.*

The Apostle Paul said:

*". . . also we have obtained an inheritance, having been predestined according to His purpose who works **all things** after the counsel of His will."*
Ephesians 1:11

*"Create in me a new, clean heart, O God, filled with clean thoughts and right desires. Don't toss me aside, banished forever from your presence. Don't take your Holy Spirit from me. Restore to me again the joy of your salvation, and make me willing to obey you. **Then I will teach your ways** to other sinners, and they—guilty like me—will repent and return to you."*
Psalm 51:10-13 (TLB)

The future is secure because God promises—when our hearts are completely His—every circumstance in our lives, including *all* we perceive as "bad," will produce an outcome that is absolutely good in His sight. It will result in our ultimate benefit, not detriment. He even takes the ashes of our past failures and transforms them into that which glorifies Him for the remainder of our futures.

We can face whatever comes each day with the absolute confidence that God is *always good, always in control, always working everything out for our ultimate good.* That means there is nothing—absolutely nothing—left for us to be afraid, worried, angry, stressed, or upset about.

Isn't God incredibly good? How can we ever doubt Him again?

> *"O taste and see that **the Lord is good;** How blessed is the man who takes refuge in Him."*
> Psalm 34:8

Sherryl

You bore our children and, for the most part, raised them. You made our house a warm and nurturing home, and fulfilled many responsibilities outside that realm as well.

You pray without ceasing. You are sensitive to the needs of others. You freely sacrifice yourself for me and all those whom you love. You don't give a thought to wrinkling your dress when hugging a youngster.

You are sincere, preferring accuracy to exaggeration. You believe clearly that what is wrong is wrong and what is right is right. You would never consider cheating on your income tax or taking advantage of another person's weakness.

It seems you never complain about your never ending day— even when I kick back after my day at the office. You have God's wisdom to speak when necessary, and His grace to just let me carry on, knowing I'm wrong at times.

You will give far more true love in your lifetime than you will ever receive.

You must be an angel.

—Daryl

6

Traveling Partners

Freedom to Love My Mate

*"Live happily with the woman you love through
the fleeting days of life, for the wife God gives you is
your **best reward** down here for all your earthly toil."*
Ecclesiastes 9:9 (TLB)

Looking back I can see an interesting sequence of events following my encounter with the Lord. I've shared about my growing hunger and thirst to know more of the God of peace, and how I eagerly returned to His Word again and again. Initially, the things He taught me focused on my personal relationship with Him, and how His ultimate purpose is to conform me to His image. Next, He revealed that He is the very essence of "goodness" and that obedience to His Word results in a joy filled life that glorifies Him.

65

As I mentioned earlier, I had assumed my new commitment would soon result in the need to change my vocation, but later discovered this was not God's priority. Instead of changing my career, He began to open my eyes to changes He wanted to make in the way I lived at home.

God Begins At Home

I understand today that for the first 12 years of marriage, I loved success and used my wife. I loved "achieving." I expected her to cope and be available whenever I needed her. As a result, I had been largely responsible for a home in which tension reigned. Sherryl and I couldn't seem to talk about even the most harmless subjects without arguing. I didn't have a clue about her needs as a woman, and no wonder since I was pouring nearly all my time and energy into building a business. Occasionally I would give her a new dress, flowers, or jewelry, hoping to convince her I loved her and soothe my conscience. I never understood that she would have preferred we just spend a little quality time together. Though she would accept the things I bought for her, I didn't understand what she was really thinking. Then one day some time after Dave's death she startled me by blurting out, "I can see that your time is the most important thing to you—and *when you don't have time for me, it can only be because I'm not important to you.*"

The shock of hearing her say she didn't feel she was important—after all the things I had provided her for more than a decade—caused my mind to race in search of something I could say to

> **I loved success and used my wife.**

convince her I really loved her. I couldn't stand the realization that for so long she had felt so unloved.

Though I was usually good at coming up with ways of justifying myself and wriggling out of tight spots, this time I couldn't find anything to offset her simple logic. How could I really love her, she reasoned, if my business, my career, and my success

I criticized her and erased her joy.

always took precedence over her? How could I really love her when I set my priorities according to what my business and my customers demanded, never by her needs? And how could any of my talk about "love" for the past 12 years be true when, even when I was with her, my mind and my heart were usually somewhere else?

As horrible as it was to admit, I knew she was right. Our family seldom ate dinner together. When she would ask if I'd be home in time for supper, I would say yes and then think nothing about coming in an hour or two late. Even then, *she* would apologize because the meal was cold. Of course, I was completely unaware of how important it was to her for us to share one meal together each day. When she finally began to open up to me, I learned that missing meals was just one of many ways *I was robbing her of one of her joys.* Instead of being a life partner who completed her and increased her happiness, I had become a life critic who perpetually criticized her and erased her joy. As God—through Sherryl—began to make me aware of my extreme self-centeredness and the effect it was having on the woman I professed to love, the pain was nearly unbearable.

God used Sherryl's words that day to begin the process of healing our relationship. But in those early days I had no idea that these new growth experiences were only the first small steps in an entire reshaping process that God would continue right up to the present.

Following that initial encounter, I could sense that He was giving me a new desire. Now I wanted to be at home with my family for dinner, a practice I continue to enjoy with rare exception. To my surprise, I discovered that making this happen often had more to do with my priorities than the time my business required to be successful.

Killing My Wife

I was totally unprepared for what occurred one spring morning as I was getting dressed for work. I was complaining—as usual—to Sherryl that my shirt wasn't perfectly starched. As I glanced out the window into the back yard, I noticed the dogs' wear and tear in one of the flower beds, so I mentioned that to her as well. Then I went on to quiz her about money she had spent on a shower gift for a friend. In other words, it was a typical morning for me.

Finally, as I was standing with my briefcase in hand, ready to leave for work, waiting for my usual good-bye kiss, Sherryl began to cry. As I watched, dumbfounded, not knowing what was wrong or what to do, her body began convulsing with sobs as she tried to stifle her sorrow and hide her tears behind her hands. I moved to her side, horrified at her anguish.

"Sherryl," I finally asked softly, "what in the world is wrong?"

Barely able to speak, she sobbed, "I just can't take it anymore."

I saw how broken and sincere she was, so after a few moments I asked, "What can't you take anymore?"

She looked at me with a countenance that reflected just how emotionally shattered she really was. Apparently my previous response over being home for dinner gave her the courage to finally share what had been tearing her apart for years. "I can't stand your continual criticism of me. I've tried as hard as I know how for the past 12 years to please you, but I just can't make you happy."

Though I was shaken by her tears and emotion, at first I wondered, "Have I really been *that* critical?" Sure, I might have come down a bit hard when requiring that our house be neat and orderly. And maybe I had been a little too fussy about the yard and my clothes. But then, as Sherryl's tears and words hit home, I began to hear myself asking why my shirt hadn't been ironed just right; why my favorite meal had not been prepared like I wanted it; why she let the kids get away with so much; how and why she spent money; and on, and on, and on.

"Still," I rationalized to myself, "didn't she know I thought everything was 99 percent good? Didn't she realize how much I appreciated her? Didn't I give her everything she wanted? Wasn't my nit-picking insignificant compared to the good things I was doing for her and our family?"

This time my usual process of self-justification was stopped dead in its tracks as she continued, *"I just wish I could die so you can marry someone else who will make you happy."*

Her words literally shook my world. In total shock I dropped my briefcase and began to silently take stock of our marriage. I vividly remembered the day on the campus of Biola University when I first saw the woman I knew I wanted as my wife. I was walking to class when the most beautiful girl I had ever seen stepped out of the library and paused under an olive tree to talk to several of her friends.

Much later—after dating, courtship, and years of marriage—I found out that life for Sherryl had not been so beautiful. But because I was too immature to understand, for years I saw only the things I wanted to see—her servant's heart, her generosity, her selfless caring for the children and me. I wasn't aware that she longed to simply have a warm, loving home. Not a huge, fancy house—but just a *home* of her own where she felt loved.

Now she literally wished she was dead. Why? So her husband could be "happier." How could I have brought her to this point of loneliness and desperation? Where had I missed the mark in our marriage? Worse yet, why didn't she know I loved her?

"Haven't I told you I love you?" I asked.

"Only when we were intimate," she said. "That tells me that you love me only for sex instead of loving me for myself."

Instead of exploding with defensiveness like I might have done before, I was taken back to that day I held my heart up to God and asked Him to take over. He was obviously answering my prayer, because now I found myself listening in quiet shame and embarrassment. God was in

> **Lord, help me to become someone who heals rather than hurts.**

the process of giving me the freedom of wanting to listen to Sherryl and to take to heart whatever she was willing to share. I put my arms around her and asked, "Why didn't you say something sooner?"

"I thought you would just get mad at me," she softly replied.

As we stood there holding each other, tears filling our eyes, neither of us could speak. Finally, realizing for the first time the enormity of what I had been doing to my wife, I prayed in desperation, "Lord, help me to change. Help me not to incessantly criticize my wife anymore. God, I don't want to have a critical spirit toward the person I say I love the most. Forgive me for nearly destroying an already broken person. Lord, because You know my heart,

You can help me to understand, to become someone who heals rather than hurts my wife. Beginning today, Lord, I don't want to criticize her or anyone else ever again."

In the days following that prayer, I began to notice more and more injunctions in God's Word against a spirit of criticism and words that hurt rather than heal. For instance:

"*. . . put . . . aside . . . abusive speech . . . .*"
Colossians 3:8

"*Let no unwholesome word proceed from your mouth, but only such a word as is good for edification.*"
Ephesians 4:29

"*Let him who means to love life and see good days refrain his tongue . . . from speaking guile.*"
1 Peter 3:10

As the Lord continued working on my heart with these verses and others, a troubling question arose in my mind: how could I have always considered murder and adultery as sins I would never commit, yet have been so free with critical comments and condemning attitudes? Was it because I did not believe a critical spirit was as bad a sin before God? Was it because there's no social or political law against it? Or was it because I didn't believe criticism and condemning words hurt others as much as murder or adultery?

Through this, God opened my eyes to a whole new perspective on the horrible sin of a critical spirit and critical words with everyone else in all my relationships.

71

> "... *the tongue is a small thing, but what enormous*
> *damage it can do. A great forest* [marriage] *can be set*
> *on fire by one tiny spark* [teasing, nit-picking, criticism,
> constant disapproval]. *And the tongue is a flame of fire.*
> *It is full of wickedness and poisons every part of the*
> *body. And the tongue is set on fire by hell itself, and can*
> *turn our whole lives into a blazing flame of destruction*
> [of our mate and kids] *and disaster.*"
>
> James 3:5-6 (TLB)

I realized that if this verse was true, it meant that my criticism was destroying—literally *killing*—my wife! No wonder my many years of criticism and nagging had worn Sherryl down to a point of utter desperation.

From that point on, I prayed that criticism, nit-picking, a critical spirit, and all my harsh words of disapproval would not only entirely disappear from my conversation, but from my attitudes as well.

Recently I was talking with one of our franchisees— also a competitive athlete—and telling him how God was helping me see the kind of trauma even one critical word can inflict on my wife. In order to drive home the gravity of a husband's criticism, I asked him to imagine what it would be like if I doubled up my fist and hit my wife full-force in the face (which, of course, I would never do). Though I might apologize, my apology wouldn't heal her

> **My criticism was destroying—literally killing—my wife.**

broken jaw. And though she would forgive me, it would take weeks, even months, for the pain to go away and the injury to heal.

This is a vivid illustration of the kind of enormous damage our words can inflict on our wives and others. Now I understand that those little critical words I used to consider "no big deal" were actually *"full of wickedness and poisons,"* with the potential to bring long-lasting, continuous pain to my wife, or even to ultimately destroy our marriage.

My #1 Customer

One day, as I was reading 1 Peter, God began to show me that not only should I seek to never criticize my wife, but also that she should be my number one "customer." In other words, as I go about my professional life in addition to my personal life, I should never put any customer or client before my spouse.

> *"You husbands likewise, live with your wives in an understanding way, as with a weaker vessel, since she is a woman; and grant her honor as a fellow-heir of the grace of life, so that your prayers may not be hindered."*
>
> 1 Peter 3:7

Even though I was more regularly coming home for dinner on time, I had been ready to jump at a moment's notice to keep my business customers happy—at the same time expecting the one "client" I professed to love the most to be satisfied with whatever time was left over. My business customers got "prime time," while my wife got very little time. And often even when I was with her I continued to be preoccupied with my "real" customers.

Gradually I began to understand that God's priority for me was that I should live with Sherryl—not my business customers—in a way that showed continual sensitivity, understanding, and consideration for her above and before all others. In essence, God was saying, "Daryl, don't bother

73

praying to me about your business or anything else if you're not sensitive toward and considerate of Sherryl's needs. I won't even hear you!"

Over the years I've learned that living with my wife "in an understanding way" includes:

• Considering her feelings and desires before accepting or even pursuing any more responsibility—especially any involvement that could mean

| Sherryl is my #1 customer! |

more of my physical or mental time away from her and the family (like serving on another board, venturing into a new business, enrolling for night school, even personal recreation).

• Not asking her to dress in a way that is uncomfortable for her.

• Not thinking only of my sexual needs, but instead considering her mood, her feelings, and her need for privacy.

• Not assuming I know what she would prefer, and not trying to change her mind once she has told me what she would like.

• Sincerely respecting her feelings and not just brushing them aside while thinking, "She's just more emotional than me. She'll get over it."

• Being careful not to hurt her feelings by complaining about small inconveniences.

• Fulfilling commitments I have made to her, such as being home for dinner as I promised, or spending quality— and quantity—time with her.

• Oh yes—and when I finally decide to let my daughter have an iguana, not just telling my wife that she shouldn't be so afraid, but showing her how I have secured every opening in the cage so there's no way the thing can ever get out!

I Need Help!

Another huge marriage-changing light came from the second chapter of Genesis:

"It is not good for the man to be alone; I will make him a helper. . . ."

Genesis 2:18

For some reason, as I thought about the meaning of this verse, a familiar childhood memory popped into my mind. Many mornings as I came to breakfast before school, my mom would include half a grapefruit on my plate. It was always one of my favorites. In relation to this passage, that memory suddenly took on new meaning. It was as though the Lord was saying to me, "Daryl, I know you've always thought of yourself as 'whole,' self-sufficient, and totally adequate. But I am *your* Creator and I am telling you that you, as a married person, are only half of a whole marriage. You can never be complete as a spouse by yourself any more than that half of a grapefruit can become whole by itself. Daryl, you're married to your other half. Only as you allow me to bring you and Sherry together can both of you experience the wholeness I have planned for you."

I began to understand that God did not intend for me to function alone; to discipline our children alone; to make decisions alone, or even to conduct my business life without any of her input. In His perfect plan, it was

I'm only half a grapefruit.

best that He bring someone alongside me to help me—to complement my weaknesses. Instead of resisting the fact that I indeed have weaknesses (and *plenty* of them), I needed to begin allowing Him to use my wife to bring about changes in areas I never thought possible.

For example, in regard to the discipline of our children, I learned that Sherryl balanced my tendency toward harsh punishment with a more reasonable treatment. I would have run our family with too much law and too little grace, with little or no input from Sherryl. She offset my severity and harshness with her

> **What a difference it made when I began to listen to Sherryl as God's best help for my life.**

gentleness and compassion. My tendency then (when our kids were younger) to restrict all their privileges actually punished Sherryl more than the kids by keeping them in the house for days at a time. Eventually, as I became more open to her perspective, Sherryl suggested we take away other privileges to make the same point. So by looking to her counsel and help, together we began making much better decisions than either of us could have made on our own.

The lesson I needed to learn, then, was that God did not intend for Sherryl or me to raise our kids alone—but together. He knew we both needed the other to balance out and temper our decisions as well as our actions.

Until I saw what the Creator was saying in Genesis concerning man's condition and his need for a helper, I didn't see the need to ask my spouse for help. After all, as the "man of the house" I believed I was supposed to have all the answers. In fact, instead of relying on her additional insight to make up for what I might not see or understand, I would criticize her for not being just like me—not realizing that God had brought us together in marriage to complete one another. What a difference it made in our relationship when, instead of being critical and resenting

Sherryl's comments, I began to listen to her as God's best help for my life.

As the Lord continues to bring us together, the more I understand what Christ meant when He said:

". . . the two shall become one flesh."
Ephesians 5:31

This remarkable phenomenon occurs when God begins supernaturally moving two people to blend their thinking, to give support to one another, and to help each other in their areas of weakness and need.

Love Is . . .

The prayer of my heart every day as I read God's Word is, "Lord, speak to me about me." As a result, new areas continually come to light in which I still need to be more aware of my wife's feelings and needs.

For example, year after year of our marriage I assumed that whatever I loved, Sherryl would love, too. If she didn't like it at first (I reasoned), she would if I exposed her to the situations I loved and if she gave them an honest try. So every year I took her fishing. But she never really seemed

> **If taking my wife bear hunting isn't love, what is?**

to get into it. Then I enthusiastically planned a bear hunt, knowing *beyond a doubt* that she would just *love* coming face-to-face with a huge wild beast she had only previously admired stuffed at a local boutique. But I just couldn't seem to convince her to go on this marvelous trip. Finally, after much persuasion, prodding, and pleading, she confessed to me, "Daryl, even though those things are fun for you, they're just not fun for me."

Wait a minute! How could it not be fun for her? *I* love bear hunting; *I* love my wife; therefore, *she* must love bear hunting too. I thought, "If taking my wife bear hunting isn't love, what is?"

However, since by now God had tuned my heart to listen, I didn't just ignore her words. I began to silently ponder what Sherryl had said: "Those things are fun for you, but they're not fun for me." Though this was a quiet statement instead of the crushing words the Lord had used before, they would prove to have another profound effect on our marriage.

Over the next few weeks they continued to echo in my head—"not fun for me." Gradually I realized that even though Sherryl didn't enjoy some of the same things I did, it was all right. God made us that way, and that if I really loved her I would not insist that she *had* to like what I did.

These thoughts, however, triggered a desire to more deeply consider what it meant to truly love my wife the way God intended. I turned again to 1 Corinthians 13— the "love chapter." There I was stopped in verse 4 by the very first definition of love: "Love is *patient* . . . ." I couldn't go on. I thought, "Patience is certainly not what I felt every time I whispered 'I love you Sherryl.'" The truth of the Scripture convicted me again. In spite of all that God had already done to heal our marriage, I realized just how selfishly I still continued to live my life in many areas. I confessed to the Lord that, more often than not, my words of love for Sherryl came only from an emotional desire that hoped to get her affection in return. I prayed that He would begin immediately to produce in me the fruit of His true love.

Today this new understanding of love causes me to often re-examine my heart when I say "I love you" to anyone. In fact, when I tell my kids I love them, I ask myself if my comments are truly a verbal affirmation of the "patience" they have experienced from me, or just empty words.

Another error in my "husband" thinking was revealed by the following verse:

"Her children arise and call her blessed; her husband also, and he praises her:"
Proverbs 31:28 (NIV)

While I admired many things about Sherryl, I seldom told her, because I always *assumed* she knew what I was thinking. I realized from this verse that a godly husband doesn't just "think" in appreciation toward his wife, but blesses his wife by regularly and frequently verbalizing his love and praise for her.

Not long ago, I was sharing with a group of businessmen in a seminar the biblical understanding of marital love and the importance of both *showing* our wives by our actions that we truly love them, and also regularly telling them how much we love and appreciate them. One man raised his hand and asked, "Is it really that important to tell our wives *every day?* Can't I just tell her once that I love and appreciate her and expect her to remember it?" For the benefit of wives everywhere I replied, "Well, would it be okay with you if she provided sex for you only once and then expected you to remember it?" He seemed to get the point.

I doubt that there's a woman alive who would not appreciate being told as often as possible that she is loved, cherished, and appreciated, provided the words are truly an expression of the definitive love in 1 Corinthians 13.

In short, I've discovered that the process of God changing and improving our marriage begins with Him changing *me*—certainly a long and difficult ordeal. Just when I think I am doing great and don't have too much

79

farther to go, He turns on another light and I begin the learning process in yet another area.

Not too long after I understood the "bear hunting lesson," I made a sincere attempt to get into shopping with my wife. One Saturday I went with her to one of her favorite boutiques (one of those stores so crammed with artificial flowers, knick-knacks, pictures, towels, and lace that it is difficult to walk around without breaking something). Needless to say, it was the last place I would have gone on my own—but I was making my best effort to take part in something she enjoyed.

As I followed her around, she stopped at a ribbon rack and began examining different colors and patterns of ribbon for a bow she wanted to make for our home. Finally she turned to me and asked, "Which one do you think is prettiest?"

Fortunately, I didn't respond in my usual manner, which would have been something insensitive like, "Just get what you want. I'm not into ribbons and it really doesn't make any difference to me."

Instead I thought, "Okay, she's really sincere and wants my opinion." So I looked over the selections and said, "I like this one."

She looked at the one I chose and then asked, "What about this other one?"

I said, "Well, I like that one, too."

So—to my amazement—she bought the one she liked, because I liked it too.

Even more significant, I saw a spark of joy in her eyes that was there simply because I was with her helping her pick out a ribbon. The more I thought about it, the more I realized that what had happened in that boutique wasn't about ribbons—it

> **Value what she values, just because she values it.**

80

was another insight God was providing to improve our marriage. Finally, after so many years of marriage on my terms, I began to see the importance of valuing what my wife values, just because she values it.

> *"Don't just think about your own affairs* [what I like], *but be interested in others, too, and in what they are doing* [what my wife likes, too]. *"*
> Philippians 2:4 (TLB)

As the refinement of this light continued and I desired to spend more time with Sherryl, I became aware of another closely-related area. Previously, I thought that loving my wife meant allowing her to watch her favorite show uninterrupted while I went off to another part of the house to watch the news. However, I began to discover that love to Sherryl also meant the assurance that *I want to be with her.* In fact, I found out she would rather be with me while I watch football than be alone watching her favorite show. Once I began to share her priority of togetherness—miracle of miracles—I began to enjoy her programs, just because she's there with me.

The Home Stress

The sheer wonder of what God had in store for us when He directed us to each other is far better than I ever imagined that first day I saw her at college. And, as I share in our *Marriage in Living Color* seminars, she is the other half of our "one flesh-ness" in the biblical and spiritual sense of the term, not just the physical. It's still a shock to me to look back to my years in the dark and realize that *I* was the source of the stress that threatened to destroy our home.

To help me remember those things I need to avoid as I desire for Christ to continue controlling my life, some time ago I wrote down the ten best (read *worst*) ways to increase the stress and anxiety in our home:

1. Criticize my wife;
2. Bring my body home but leave my mind at work;
3. Withhold praise from my kids;
4. Hate my job;
5. Believe life has dealt me a poor hand—I'm a victim;
6. Assume our children are my wife's responsibility alone;
7. Be lazy;
8. Allow my kids to say and do whatever they want;
9. Don't talk to my wife—grunting is sufficient;
10. And, to top it all off, expect sex.

Wive's Words

This is a particularly difficult chapter for me to conclude, because God has used my wife to introduce me to so many new freedoms. However, I'll summarize with this. Though we may deny it or ignore it, our wives really do know us best. They see us as we really are on a daily basis, and I believe they are God's special messengers to tell us—kindly and confidentially—the truth about ourselves. Their words of insight and wisdom can save our reputations, our careers, our family relationships, perhaps even our lives.

It is imperative, then, that if we truly desire for our wives to help us, we need to begin by telling them we need and appreciate their insights, their critiques, their words of advice—no matter how much hearing them might hurt.

Then we need to ask the kinds of questions that will allow our wives to share their honest opinions with us. Questions like:

- Am I easy to talk to, especially about me?
- Will our children remember me for my kindness, patience, and apologies when I was wrong?
- Do I always have to be right?
- Do you feel my career, hobby, or recreation is more important to me than you?
- Am I too critical, and if so, what are some examples?
- Where does my pride get in the way of the best interests of you, our family, and our marriage?

One final note: If you're going to ask, you had better be ready for the answers. After all, God has given us our wives as our greatest agents for change.

This has certainly been my experience as the Lord has continued to use Sherryl's words to expose the bondage of my self-love and to introduce me to an ever-increasing freedom to truly love my mate.

". . . she is worth more than precious gems! Her husband can trust her, and she will richly satisfy his needs. She will not hinder him but help him all her life."
Proverbs 31:10-12 (TLB)

Searching for a
God that Works

The world offers a shopping list of gods, each boasting a better way of life to those who would believe. But which one really works?

·   The *Pride* god promises *"I'll keep you lookin' good"*— but he seems to always keep someone looking better than me.

·   The *Money* god claims *"more of me is all you need"*— but none of his believers, I know, ever have enough.

·   The *Fight for Your Rights* god maintains *"you must be in control"*—but his entire congregation seems to be so stressed out.

Then there's the *Living God* who says *"my peace I give to you"* (John 14:27). But He doesn't *appear* to work either. Most who claim to belong to Him always appear so unhappy.

Is there a God that works? Can you show me one?

Do our kids see one?

                                            —D.K.

7

Road Kill

Freedom to Show Grace to My Children

"He is like a father to us, tender and sympathetic to those who reverence Him."
Psalm 103:13 (TLB)

As I shared in the previous chapter, God has used my wife in tremendous ways to change not only my priorities, but my outward behavior as well. Aside from our personal relationship, the other area of greatest change came as the result of another penetrating question: "Do you want your children to leave home thinking they could never please you?"

For most of their early years there was no reason why my children would have wanted to be like me. I can't believe how blind I was to the negative impact I was having on my kids.

I was constantly miffed at my older son for making a mess when he worked on his cars. I cheered on my younger son in his school sports, but always pointed out later how he could have done better. Kim, our middle child, was outgoing and on occasion would enjoy inviting large groups of her friends to our home. But usually I tried to discourage her from having so many for fear they would make a mess. Shelli—our youngest—was spared at least some of what the older children had to endure because she was still quite young when God began showing me that I was a lousy example of fatherhood.

Grace From a New Roof

Though my relationship with Sherryl was steadily improving, my poor fatherly interaction with our children did not become a spiritual issue until one day when Sherryl and I arrived home after attending our company's national convention. No sooner had we pulled into the driveway than we were met by our oldest son, who began sharing his excitement over something he had done for me while we were gone.

Greg proudly and enthusiastically led us to our pool storage shed. It was just a shack, really, behind a hill and out of sight from everything else. As he triumphantly pointed to the shed, I could see that he had completely ripped off its perfectly usable (though slightly leaky) flat roof and replaced it with a brand new A-frame structure. All I had asked him to do was fix a small leak—at most a $10 to $15 job. Immediately I reacted to the waste of money and my anger began a slow boil. "Build an expensive

> **Do you want your children to think they can never please you?**

mountain A-frame roof on a hidden pool shed?" I thought. "How ridiculous could a person be?"

The words, "Why did you do *that*?" had barely escaped my lips when I noticed on the ground a yellow charge receipt from my own credit card. I snatched up the charge slip and discovered that the unwanted, unnecessary, ridiculous roof had cost me almost $400! At the same moment, someone in the house called Greg to the telephone, so I quickly wheeled around to follow.

Sherryl, who had been quietly observing my growing anger said, "Wait a minute Daryl, where are you going?"

"Where do you think I'm going," I shot back. "I'm going up to the house to ask Greg why in the world he would ever do such a stupid thing!"

"Why?" Sherryl calmly asked.

"Look at this!" I persisted. "How in the world could Greg do something this wasteful?"

I was angry—angry at Greg, and angry at myself for leaving a credit card at home instead of just giving him $20 to fix the leak. I wanted to grab my son and shake him hard, but he had been called to the phone before I had a chance, and that made me even more angry.

I was trapped in a horrible prison. As a perfectionist who worshipped the god of materialism, I was always conscious of every dollar my family spent. *Though I didn't mind wasting money on myself, I sure didn't want anyone else wasting it.* Now I was faced with nearly half a thousand dollars down the drain *for nothing.* On top of that, Greg had left the mess for me to clean up, and I hated messes. Right then I felt a desperate need to bite something, shake something, kick something, or tell someone off.

That's when Sherryl asked me, "What are you going to say to him?"

"What do you think I'm going to say to him?" I snapped. "I'm going to tell him what I think about this roof and make sure nothing like this ever happens again. I need this new roof like I need a hole in my head."

As I started for the house, my wife had already decided she was not going to let me continue destroying my son. "Daryl," she called, stopping me in my tracks, "have you considered that the money is already spent, and that Greg's only motivation was to please you?"

Then, as I was trying to sort through what she had just said, Sherryl's next question hit me with the force of a sledgehammer: "Daryl, do you want your son to leave home thinking he could never please you?"

I stood there, quietly, for what seemed a long time, as God used Sherryl's words to open my heart to the truth. For 16 years of Greg's life, I had griped at him and seldom, if ever, complimented him. Now I had come within mere minutes of hurting him even further. Realizing the damage my anger could have done, I started to weep. Inside I began to desperately cry out for the Lord to change me. In a matter of moments my anger began to be replaced by appreciation for my son's motives. I went from wanting to shake my boy to hugging my wife.

"Thanks," I whispered to her, realizing she had saved me from devastating my son. I silently thanked God for the phone call that had taken him away, and especially for my wife's wisdom. My relationship with Greg, and eventually everyone else in my life, would forever be changed because of God's wisdom to Sherryl, and her courage to tell me the truth in love.

Tough Questions

During this time in our lives the older kids were in junior and senior high, and since both schools were on my way to work it was easy for me to take them every morning. This meant that we spent as much as 20 or 30 minutes together in the car each day. Once we ran out of small talk about grades, sports, friends, and social events, I began asking them to level with me about life, their perceptions of me, and our family. This was another significant change that began at Dave's bedside. The

> **It is important for my kids to *feel* I *respect* them as well as *hear* me say *I love them.***

Lord was continuing to replace my old defensiveness with a deep desire to know and experience truth. As vividly as God had spoken to me through my wife, I was curious to know what further insights I might gain if I really began to listen to my children and respect what they had to say. So as we traveled I would ask them questions like these:

- Do you think I love your brother or sister more than you?
- Do you feel I'm more strict with you than with the others?
- Do you think I live the way I'm teaching you to act?
- Do you think I'm a happy person, or a critical person?
- Do you think something in my life is really more important to me than the Lord? If so, what is it?
- What one thing do you want to transfer from my life into yours?
- Do you want to be at all like me? Why or why not?
- How will you treat your kids differently from the way I've treated you?
- What one thing would you like me to change about myself?
- Do you think I'm too strict? Not strict enough?

- How is our family different from your friends' families?
- What changes have you seen God make in my life that you would like Him to make in yours, too?
- Do you think my business is more important to me than you—or Mom?
- Do you feel I respect you, or just put up with you?
- Do you think I'm too proud to say I'm sorry?

What I learned during those morning school rides often brought tears of conviction from the tough things my kids would share. However, as time passed and I continued to listen for truth, I could tell that our relationship was, slowly but surely, changing—from one of frequent disrespectful arguing to one of a sincere love *and respect* for each other.

Today I understand that respectful listening is a big part of true love. It is far more important that my kids, and my wife, feel I respect them because I sincerely listen to them rather than just telling them I love them.

Freedom From Arguing

Arguing was not just an occasional event in our family; it was the usual way we interacted on any point of disagreement. I'll never forget the day God revealed to me through the following verses that arguing anytime, with anyone, about anything, is counter-productive.

> *"To quarrel . . . is foolish . . . ."*
> Proverbs 11:12 (TLB)

> *"Pride leads to arguments . . . ."*
> Proverbs 13:10 (TLB)

92

Arguments usually start over dual (or dueling) perceptions of what's true, but are soon replaced by two prideful demands to be right. Because it becomes a contest of "wills" rather than a contest for "truth," arguing can never bring agreement.

One day I was in the kitchen arguing, attempting to make a point with one of my teenagers, when I realized that in trying to gain ground logically I was losing ground relationally. At that moment, the reality of those verses stopped me in the middle of our heated discussion. I kept quiet for a moment as I thought about what was happening. Then I said, "What I'm doing right now God says is absolutely foolish. I want to ask His forgiveness and apologize to you for arguing and make a commitment to God and you to never argue again. I'll always love to talk with you and offer my best advice. But I never want to be foolish and hurt our relationship again."

As the years passed, our truthful exchanges, without arguing, continued as one of our new family traditions. I was acutely aware that God was using these discussions to change me, but I had no idea how deeply they were affecting my kids until shortly before my oldest daughter Kim was married. We were standing in the kitchen, reflecting back on our many long talks, when I asked, "As you move into your new home, what is the most important thing you will remember from our relationship?"

> I realized that in trying to gain ground logically I was losing ground relationally.

She thought for a moment and replied, "The fact that you listened to me."

She had never mentioned this before, so I asked her why my listening to her was so important.

"When you listened," she said, "it gave me confidence that any time I asked you about something that was important to me, you thoroughly heard me and considered my request. I could see that *what was important to me was important to you.* I accepted your answer as being in my best interest, because I knew you had really understood how important it was to me."

I silently praised God again, "Thank you, Lord, for the miraculous way you replaced my defensiveness and arguing with a new desire to listen."

"I Want Your Peace."

When my oldest son was growing up he was enamored of new cars, nice clothes, steak on the menu—everything associated with "expensive." His love for material things deeply concerned me. I didn't want to see him fall prey to the false god of materialism, whose only reward (as I well knew) was "enough is never enough" and a legacy of stress-filled days bolstered by tranquilizers.

I prayed a long time for the right opportunity to talk with him. Finally, one evening we were alone in the car on our way home from the office and the time seemed right.

"So . . . Greg," I began. "If you could choose to take one thing from my life and transfer it into your own when you establish your home four or five years from now, what would you want most?"

Inside, I knew he would answer like a typical teenager and say, "Your money." His answer, I thought, would be a perfect opportunity for me to discuss the subject. Imagine how surprised I was when he said . . . nothing. Total silence, for at least four or five minutes.

"What are you thinking?" I asked. "Just go ahead and blurt it out."

"I'm still thinking," he said.

When several more minutes passed and he still hadn't answered, I decided to relax and keep driving, giving him as much time as he wanted. Of course, I couldn't figure out what was taking him so long since the answer seemed to be so obvious. But eight minutes—ten minutes—even more time passed.

> **Do my kids want to know my God?**

Finally, as we stopped at a traffic light, I asked again, "Greg, do you know yet?"

"Yes, I know." After another long pause he finally said, *"Your peace."*

I was stunned! As we drove on it was all I could do to keep the car on the road as my eyes began to fill with tears of gratitude. I remembered the many years when the only "peace" I knew came in a capsule form, when my life had nothing I would have wanted him to follow.

"I see you with material things," Greg went on, "but you've got one thing more important to me than all those things. You've got peace."

That's when one of the most tearful praises to God that I can ever remember welled up within me: "Because the God of Peace met and began to change me that day in 1973, today, my kids want to know my God." How can I ever thank Him enough?

Following this incident the Lord continued to provide me many more opportunities to reveal His life-changing peace—opportunities that often came when I least expected them.

"Thanks, Dad."

One spring morning Doug and I were hunting in Arizona. As we sat near each other in the bush with our rifles ready, the game we were stalking suddenly appeared.

Greg and our guide were only a few paces away, and all of us knew it was Doug's turn to prove his marksmanship.

"Go ahead," I whispered to Doug, "it's your shot."

As the animal came within a stone's throw, Doug eased up out of his camouflage, took careful aim, pulled the trigger . . . and missed. Missed clean, in fact. The animal took off unscathed, and Doug was left holding his rifle, facing embarrassment in front of the three people he most wanted to impress: his father, his brother, and the guide he had grown up idolizing. I could instantly relate to Doug's agony, since I had suffered similar embarrassing situations. Our good-natured guide—who stood six-foot-six and loved to tease and joke with my boys—got up from his cover and strode over in his dusty chaps, weathered hat, and cowboy boots.

"Doouug," he drawled with a big smile, "How'd you miss that easy shot? He was right in front of you! Why, Doug! I'm disappointed in ya'!"

Doug began to stammer, "Uh . . . uh . . . I didn't really have a good shot at him, and . . . uh . . . uh . . . that bush was in my way, and . . . the wind was blowing . . . and . . . "

Again I acutely felt my son's agony. After all, where did Doug get the idea he had to be perfect? The unfolding episode instantly brought to mind all the years of my own excuses, defensive letters to customers, and self-justification to my family and business associates. Not long ago I would have jumped on Doug's missed shot with a statement like, "Doggone it, Doug! You couldn't have had a better shot, and you missed! We spent all this money to come here and you can't even hit a target only a few feet away!"

But, thanks to the Lord, I was beginning to understand how cruel that would have been. Now instead of being critical I found myself feeling a new compassion, longing to help my son. I waited for my first chance to talk to

Doug alone. As the four of us walked back to the Jeep, I motioned for him to stay back with me while Greg and the guide continued walking.

"Doug," I whispered, "wait here."

"Why?" he asked in an angry and defensive tone.

"Just hold back, Doug," I said. "I know how you feel."

"What do you mean?" he asked, still very upset.

"You feel like you've embarrassed yourself in front of the whole world," I said. "I know, because I've been there. But I want you to know that the freedom I've found in the Lord means I don't have to be the best shot anymore. I can't begin to tell you what a relief that is to me. For most of my life I felt like I had to be the best at everything. But now I'm free to just do my best without having to be the best at anything. And Doug, you don't have to be the best at anything, either, because God loves you and accepts you just the way you are. Whether you hit that animal dead center or missed it by a mile means nothing in terms of my love and respect for you. You are important to me no matter what."

I was surprised at my own words, because they didn't sound like the old me, and they came without effort or strain.

As we continued walking toward the Jeep about ten yards behind the others, there

> **I'm free to just do my best without having to be the best.**

were several minutes of complete silence. Then I felt my son's arm reach around my shoulders and hug me. I looked into his eyes and saw that they were watery, but not with anger. He quietly said, "Thanks, Dad."

As we drove back to the ranch, I was overwhelmed by the realization that my radically changed attitude was the result of my Heavenly Father's amazing grace, that only a few years earlier, showed me that when I fail I'm still okay.

Now I was privileged with the opportunity to introduce my son to that same freedom rather than being another source of stress.

Moment of Truth

Another unexpected opportunity occurred not long ago right in front of our home. I was leaving for work in a brand new car—so new, it didn't yet have a license plate. Greg had just pulled out behind me in his car when I realized I had not set the alarm at home, so I braked and stuck my head out the window to ask Greg if he had set it. That's when I suddenly saw—and felt—him crash into me. Two nice, shiny cars were now damaged—his front end and my rear end.

My mind was filled with disbelief and knee-jerk reactions: "Did this really happen? How could Greg run into my new car? Wasn't he paying attention? This will cost me thousands of dollars!"

But then I also realized, "This is a moment of truth, right here in the middle of the street. I'm either going to contradict everything my son has heard from me, or I'm going to affirm what I've said by showing that the one true God—not my old god of materialism and love for new things—is now my controlling passion."

As I opened the car door and walked back to Greg, the prayer on my heart was, "Lord, please fill me with Yourself and Your thoughts. Please don't let my old ways get the victory and destroy both my testimony and my peace."

"Greg," I said, "Come here." As he walked toward me I met him with a smile and gave him a huge hug, right there in the street, in front of my neighbors. Then I said, "I want you to know that these cars are not what life is all about. We'll get them fixed. I love you."

Finding myself at peace in the midst of two wrecked cars (for me that was true freedom!) I silently prayed,

"Thank You, thank You, Lord. Your grace is *real*—not just words to a song I sing in church."

Freedom From Sweating the Small Stuff

Today, my children are grown, and I'm thankful for all that God has done to bring His love into our relationships. In addition to the major areas I've shared, along the way He's even given me freedom over the small stuff. For instance He freed me from believing that because my hair was short, my boys' hair should be short too, and any haircut longer than mine was wrong; from thinking if my daughter wanted to wear shoes that to me looked like combat boots, that too was wrong; and ditto for more than one hole pierced in my daughter's ears, and so on. He's also freed me from being concerned about what my friends might think; that I might look like I had lost control, or that I wasn't a good Christian parent.

> I praise God for the freedom to love my children just the way they are.

Today, I *know* that our relationship with the Lord has nothing to do with how our kids look or dress or, for that matter, what our friends may think. Of course, this does not negate our biblical responsibility to "train up" our children in the Lord. But it gives us tremendous freedom to concentrate on those things that really are important— our kids' relationship with Him, moral purity, honesty, and integrity.

How I praise God for the freedom today to love my children just the way they are.

> ". . . *your children like olive plants around your table. Behold, for thus shall the man be blessed who fears the LORD.*"
>
> Psalm 128:3-4

Skydiving

Several years ago, I climbed aboard a small aircraft and flew up through a layer of clouds to 12,500 feet, where the pilot and an instructor gave me a thumbs up sign meaning, "Okay—jump out!" Then, harnessed together, we moved to the opening and dove into space. We continued to free fall at 120 miles per hour for nearly a minute, then pulled the rip cord and slowed our otherwise fatal descent to a stand-up landing. My boys (who also jumped) called it "a rush." Sherryl, who didn't jump, called it "a brain lapse." I called it an incredible experience; in fact, I couldn't wait to do it again.

Since then I've continued to ask myself this question: Do I trust God with my life as much as I trusted that instructor? And do I trust His parachute—no matter what my free fall in life— to land me gently on my feet? Seems that's what Habakkuk was referring to when he said:

> *"He has made my feet like hinds' feet, and makes me walk on my high places."*
> Habakkuk 3:19

8

The Navigator

Freedom from Believing It's All Up to Me

"The Lord will accomplish what concerns me."
Psalm 138:8

In spite of my best efforts to hold it off, my fiftieth birthday finally arrived. As we celebrated this landmark event, one of my sons asked me, "Dad, now that you're 50, what's the first thing that comes to your mind?"

I only had to think for a moment before replying, "I can see now that *I worried about a lot in life I didn't have to.*"

Every Sunday morning on our way to church we pass a small office complex where a neon sign on one of the units flashes the message, "Power Resumés!" The implication, of course, is that all a job hunter needs to do is let a professional employment agency prepare the facts

> **So much of life is given to worry —and it's all for nought.**

correctly, and a job is guaranteed. That sums up the way I used to think: I had to depend on my own "power" to make things happen.

For all my life prior to Dave's death, I looked at life thinking I had to achieve most, if not all, of what God says *He freely gives.* I believed it was primarily up to *my* education, *my* ingenuity, *my* persuasiveness, *my* tenacity, *my* cleverness, *my* ability to get what I wanted out of life.

God Gives

In the first chapter of the book of Joshua, God told Joshua, the leader of the nation of Israel, at least five times that the "promised land" (the reality of God's best) was not something the children of Israel could obtain through their own efforts. Rather, it was a *gift* that God was going to give His people. Consider:

Joshua 1:2   "*. . . the land which I am **giving** to them . . .*"
        1:3   "*. . . I have **given** it to you . . .*"
        1:6   "*. . . the land which I swore . . . to **give** them.*"
        1:13   "*. . . God . . . will **give** you this land . . .*"
        1:15   "*. . . the land . . . the Lord . . . is **giving** them.*"

As a young adult, I often taught Sunday school lessons and Bible studies that dealt with what God promises to give His children if they will only trust Him with their lives. But then on Monday morning I would continue living my business life in ways that were self-serving, proud, and often manipulative.

In those dark years I honestly thought my ways were just "good business." For example, in order to sell a new franchise to a prospective buyer, I would highlight the companies that were doing well while ignoring those that were doing poorly. I also felt any kind of threat was justifiable to collect money owed to me.

But then God gave me some profound insights into just how different His ways were from my own.

> *"This book of the law shall not depart from your mouth, but you shall meditate on it day and night, so that **you may be careful to do** according to all that is written in it; for **then you will make your way prosperous**, and then you will have success."*
> Joshua 1:8

God was essentially telling Joshua, "*You don't have to put a good 'spin' on anything.* All you have to do is live by My Word, and *I'll give* you the success I want you to have. I'll win all your battles if you'll just follow Me."

In chapter 6, God went on to clarify that Joshua's success had more to do with his obedience than with his own abilities or efforts:

> *"I'll show you my power when you come up against Jericho's wall,"* He said. *"All you have to do is walk around it seven times and shout on the seventh lap (obey me). Then the walls will come down right in front of you (I'll personally bring them down)."*
> (author's paraphrase)

This way of living is exactly opposite from the collective "success" voices we hear all around us today. "You can do anything you want," they shout, "if *you* just try hard enough!" In fact, when I fail to trust the Lord, I hear the same "it's all up to me" voices again: "I *need* to say (whatever) to sell my product."

"I *need* to change something about (my mate) so I can be happier."

"I *need* to change (my kids) or *they'll* never hold their marriages together."

However, the Word of God speaks in sharp contrast to what our old natures believe. All God asks of us is that we turn from our *"it's all up to me"* mentality and meditate "day and night" on His Words, with a desire to obey them in all that we do.

". . . then you will make your way prosperous,
and then you will have success."
Joshua 1:8

As God has continued to reveal His ways of blessing and freedom, I have become increasingly uncomfortable with many of my past methods. No longer can I, with a clear conscience, shade the good or bad about anything in order to make a deal. No longer am I comfortable trying to put a good look on my bad used

> **Success has more to do with our obedience to God than our abilities, education, and efforts.**

car in order to sell it. No longer do I feel right about trying to wriggle out of a promise or agreement I made in the past because it has become uncomfortable to me in the present. And, of course, no longer can I conveniently tell my wife I'll be home for dinner at the time she wants me to, then show up an hour or two later.

> **Lord, help me to see the things I'm still trying to do for myself that You've promised to do for me.**

Some time ago, I told a very good friend that I could not go along with a plan he was proposing because I felt it was not entirely honest. I went on to tell him about the changes God was making in my life, and that continuing in this new freedom was far more important to me than the "gain" that might come from again believing that my business success depends on me and my ingenuity.

"Daryl," he replied, "you just don't realize that's what you have to do out here these days to be successful."

That was exactly the kind of thinking that caused all the pain and stress during my nail-biting, knots-in-the-pit-of-the-stomach, tranquilizer-popping years.

I thank God that today He's planted within me this simple prayer: *"Lord, help me to believe that all I need in life is mine through simple trust and obedience, not through my own power. Lord, help me to see the things I'm still trying to do for myself that You've promised to do for me."*

As I've continued my search to know God better, I've been amazed at all He gives to His obedient children.

Wisdom

"For the Lord gives wisdom; from his mouth come knowledge and understanding."
                    Proverbs 2:6

God promises to give His children all the insight and discernment we need to manage our families and businesses in a way that brings glory to Him—if we will just meditate on His Word and desire to grow in His character.

Peace

> *"My peace I **give** to you."*
> John 14:27

God promises to give real *peace* to anyone who asks and obeys Him. This is the essence of *my* personal journey in Christ! ***God has given me a peace I had tried—and failed—to find through my own efforts .***

Grace

> *"But He **gives** a greater grace."*
> James 4:6

God also gives His children grace—grace greater than all our needs! It's not up to us to somehow prepare ourselves to be able to withstand things that may come our way.

Thinking back, my cousin Dave's experience was a perfect example of God's sustaining grace. God gave him all the grace he needed even when he was on the threshold of death. When I go back and re-read the poem Dave wrote from his deathbed, I'm once again awed and encouraged by the incredible example of faith and the measure of grace God gave him.

Contentment

> *"Blessed are those who hunger and thirst for*
> *righteousness* [obedience], *for they shall be satisfied."*
> Matthew 5:6

It is not necessary for us to change our circumstances in order to be happy. No external change can produce the contentment God alone can give.

Security

> *"He will cover you with His pinions* [feathers],
> *and under His wings you may seek refuge . . . For He*
> *will give His angels charge concerning you, to guard*
> *you in all your ways."*
> Psalm 91:4, 11

God even promises to give us protection and security according to His *perfect will*.

It was in this very important area of security that my dear wife, Sherryl, believed God's Word and experienced His freedom before I did. In fact, her example of deep faith has continued through the years to be a great encouragement to me.

While we were in the process of trying to have a fourth child, Sherryl suffered two consecutive miscarriages. The doctor advised us that a third miscarriage would likely pose a serious risk to her health. Sherryl and I talked it over, but she still wanted to try again. I kept raising the question of her physical health, but to no avail. She really wanted another baby.

After the second miscarriage, Sherryl was scheduled for minor surgery. The doctor suggested that if we wanted to eliminate the potential risk of a future pregnancy, he could take care of the matter at the same time. His suggestion, however, was so painful we didn't even discuss it. Finally, the day arrived and we drove to the hospital. Sherryl checked in and was placed in a wheelchair in the waiting room. Several minutes later the doctor approached me with a consent form and said, "If you want to go ahead with the other, you will need to sign this form." He pointed to a blank line where my signature would result in ending any possibility we would ever again have children.

I asked Sherryl what she wanted to do, and she began to sob. Then, just before the attendants wheeled her down the hallway, she said, "Daryl, I still want another child very much—but I may be too emotional right now to make the right decision. I'll trust the final decision to you."

What? I thought as they took her away, *I have to make the decision? Lord, if ever I've wanted You to actually appear and tell me what to do—now is the time!* For several moments I felt paralyzed, caught between the proverbial rock and a hard place. I tried to reason through my alternatives. *If I don't sign the form and later Sherryl's health is seriously affected, I will never forgive myself. However, if I make the decision to eliminate any chance for my wife to have another child, will she ever forgive me?* Finally I decided that her life was most important, and I signed the form.

Though I knew the doctor had told Sherryl of my decision, nearly a month passed before I had the nerve to mention the subject. Finally, one day when we were away together for the weekend, I nervously brought it up. "Sherryl," I tentatively asked, "the doctor told you about the decision I made, didn't he?"

"Yes," she said.

Fearfully, I continued, "How do you feel about what I did?"

"Daryl," she replied, "God gave me peace that if I would submit the final decision to you, as He asks me to, *He would never allow you to make a mistake with my life.*" Then she smiled and hugged me. I was immediately overwhelmed with the enormity of Sherryl's faith. She was completely at *peace* and knew the freedom that comes from believing that God gives her His security in exchange for her simple obedience.

About two more weeks passed, then one day, seemingly out of the blue, Sherryl said, "I know why God had you make that decision. It's because I believe He has another child somewhere in this world He wants us to love."

Today, that other child is our beautiful daughter Shelli, whom God brought to us in a totally miraculous way when she was only two days old.

But Is What God Gives Enough?

God in His great goodness answers yet another of the "old self's" anxieties: "If I really depend *totally* on Him, will I be completely satisfied with what He gives me?" The Israelites apparently had the same fear. Consider how God described the promised land to Moses.

> *"It is a land where . . . nothing is lacking."*
> Deuteronomy 8:9 (TLB)

We are often tempted to think like the Israelites: "I still need more than what God says is enough." Perhaps, when we see others who *appear* to not have enough, we are tempted to doubt even more.

Psalm 34:9-10 reads:

> "*O fear the Lord, you His saints; For to those who fear Him, **there is no want**. The young lions do lack and suffer hunger; But they who seek the Lord **shall not be in want of any good thing**.*"

Meditate on this promise. Ask God to clearly and specifically show you what He meant by the words "no want." Here is another wonderful, life-liberating discovery:

> **God promises to make us wholly satisfied with what He has given us.**

God never promises to give us so much that we can see we'll never run out. Instead, He promises to make us emotionally and spiritually satisfied with what He has given us.

So our good and gracious God gives us what He knows is best for us today. At the same time, He removes our selfish drive for more, as well as our fear of not having enough for tomorrow. Isn't God good?

Trying to Be My Own God

Not long ago, my 16-year-old daughter totaled the car she was driving. We were extremely thankful that she and her friend were unhurt. The next evening, however, we found ourselves helping her deal with the trauma that goes with this kind of experience. "Now how am I going to get to school?" she sobbed. "I just don't know what I am going to do!" More tears. "How will I know if the next car I drive is safe?" More sobbing. "*I just can't handle all this stress!*" Finally, a cloudburst of tears.

I listened for some time, then replied as calmly as I could, "Shelli, the reason you are so stressed and unhappy is because you're trying to be your own parent."

I explained to her that God had given her parents who loved her and who were prepared (as God enables) to handle these kinds of concerns for her. I told her that we had already begun thinking and praying about the things that were troubling her mind. And then I suggested, "If you will just trust us with all the things you are worried about, your stress and tears will go away. God never intended for you to carry this weight yourself. That's why He gave you parents."

Later that evening, I was thinking back over what I had said to Shelli, and my words began to speak *even louder to me* about my own trust in the Lord. I had told Shelli, "You're trying to be your own parent." Now that statement caused me to wonder how many times my Heavenly Father has tried to impress on me the same reality. Perhaps He has spoken to you about this same thing.

When the Lord sees us worried and unhappy, how many times has He tried to say, "You know all your stress and unhappiness would go away if you would just stop trying to be your own god. I love you, and nothing can separate you from My care and concern. I never intended for you to carry all this weight yourself. That's why I (your Heavenly Father) gave you My Son (Jesus Christ)."

"Be still, and know that I am God."
Psalm 46:10 (NIV)

Dying vs. Trying

God brings us a mighty freedom by providing us with *everything*—even our change of character—to glorify Him. But don't we still need to work hard at being a good Christian?

I used to think so. But let's consider what the Bible really tells us:

113

*"Always carrying about in the body **the dying** of Jesus, that the life of Jesus also may be manifested in our body."*

2 Corinthians 4:10

*"But if by the Spirit you are **putting to death** the deeds of the body, you will live."*

Romans 8:13

The Apostle Paul was saying that his progressive transformation into the image of Christ—that which we would call maturing in Christ—did not come about through his hard work or personal effort. He did not say, ". . . though you are dying to the deeds of the body you still need to work hard at being a good Christian." Instead, he simply said, "If you are dying, 'you will live.' " That means that when we die to self (truly give up what we want and desire what God wants), God automatically manifests Himself through us.

Several years ago, Sherryl and I were eagerly looking forward to spending a weekend together when, completely unforeseen to us, we had to make a late change in our plans. Instead of enjoying a special time alone, it became necessary to help someone else with a problem. My first reaction was a feeling of resentment toward those posing the inconvenience. For several days, no matter how hard I tried to camouflage my true feelings, Sherryl could see I was unhappy. In fact, my feelings soon began to grow into bitterness. Finally, after several days of struggling, I asked the Lord to help me understand why I was so unhappy. Once I *really wanted to know,* the Lord caused me to see the real reason: my old, selfish "will" was back in control.

I immediately sensed a growing resurgence of the desire I first knew at my cousin's hospital bed—I do not want my life to be controlled any longer by my old ugly self. In fact, I have grown to hate my old ways with a consuming passion.

That morning, I bowed my head and confessed my wrong attitude to the Lord. No sooner had I prayed then I felt myself coming alive with a whole new outlook. My resentment was

> **The hard work in trying to be a good Christian comes from keeping our old self alive.**

replaced with a desire to spend the weekend helping someone else, and I began looking forward to a spiritually rewarding time together. Instead of seeing the circumstance as an interruption to my schedule, I could see God was giving us a wonderful opportunity, in His perfect timing, to be an encouragement to others.

Please keep in mind that I didn't do any "work" to somehow conjure up this new attitude. Certainly there was a battle being waged in my flesh, but it was a battle simply to die to my old self and to consider myself alive to God (see Romans 6:11-14). Once *I died*, God's Spirit, who is already in me (see Galatians 2:20) was released to manifest Himself through me.

Our natural longing to "work hard" in trying to be a "good Christian" comes from allowing, or perhaps even *wanting*, to keep part of our old self alive while presenting the right spiritual appearance. This effort is about as successful as trying to apply an adhesive bandage in the shower. God says, *for as long as we're just trying to manipulate the way our old nature appears on the outside, we can never really change.*

> *"It is* [only] *the* **Spirit** *who gives life; the flesh* [human effort] *profits nothing."*
> John 6:63

> *"I am the vine . . . without me you can do nothing."*
>
> John 15:5 (NKJV)

Today, when I feel like I'm having to work hard at being a "good Christian," I am reminded in my spirit that I'm *not* considering myself dead to self and alive to God. It is an indication that I need to "die" anew to some remnant of the old self-life in me.

If, for example, I arrive home after work and my wife wants to talk while I *(selfishly)* want to relax and watch TV, I find it just more of the old "hard work" to try to chat with her. (It's even *harder* work trying to convince her I'm listening when I'm really trying to follow the score of the ball game!) But if, at that first moment, I realize I need to consider

> **If I'm not experiencing God's peace— I'm not dead yet!**

myself dead to my selfishness *(what I want to do)* and desire to be like the Lord *(putting others first)*, my new nature from Him will take over and, as a result, chatting and sharing with my wife will become effortless, natural, and enjoyable.

This freedom completely changes our understanding of what the Christian life is all about. Our old focus was "I just want to live for the Lord," believing we needed to continually work harder at doing the things God wanted us to do. Now our heartfelt cry is, "I just want to *die* for the Lord."

> *"I have been crucified with Christ; and it is **no longer I who live**, but Christ lives in me; and the life which I now live in the flesh I live by faith in the Son of God, who loved me, and delivered Himself up for me."*
>
> Galatians 2:20

If we are failing as Christians to experience any of God's abundant promises (wisdom, grace, peace, a sense of security, contentment, freedom), *it's not because we're not **trying** enough—but because we're not **dying** enough!*

The Sin of Perfection

Perfection as a standard has ruined many potentially good businesses. More important, it has defeated millions of wonderful people and destroyed numerous good homes.

The need to be perfect is one of Satan's most destructive lies—just consider a few of the consequences:

- *I'm always mad and embarrassed with myself because I can never achieve it.*

- *I'm always frustrating everyone else around me because I expect it of them.*

- *I'm always critical because everyone else appears to keep letting me down.*

- *I'm always defensive with those who try to help because just their offer seems only to expose more of my failures.*

- *I always feel guilty because I can never become who I think I should be.*

- *I can never really believe God is good because I continue to be so miserable.*

—D.K.

Environment Control Building Maintenance Company, Home Office Staff, October , 1995. Daryl is in the denim shirt in the back row.

Glenn Ranch, S.E. Arizona, 1995
Daryl and Sherryl Kraft

Fishing Lodge at Hakai, British Columbia August, 1996 (left to right): Greg Kraft, Clarence Henderson, Gerry Kraft, Daryl Kraft, Ralph Kraft, Al Seevers, and Doug Kraft

Three Generations fishing in British Columbia: Daryl, his dad Ralph, and his son Doug

The Kraft Family, December, 1996, at Lake Shasta, N. Calif. : Shelli, Wendy, Doug, Hunter, Daryl, Kevin, Matthew, Kim, Katie, Michael, and Sherryl

Daryl's Grandchildren December, 1996: (left to right) Matthew, Katie, Nikki, Michael, Hunter and Jessica

Greg Kraft with his wife Cheryl, and their daughters Jessica and Nikki in the Kraft backyard, April 1996.

Daryl at headquarters in Anaheim, California, 1995

9

Comprehensive and Collision—No Deductible

Freedom from the Need to Be Perfect

*"He knows our frame; He remembers that **we are dust.**"*

Psalm 103:14 (NKJV)

Several years ago I was discussing with one of my office staff a particularly difficult problem we encountered at our recent convention. The tension seemed to build as we analyzed what had gone wrong. Finally I said something I had never said before, which, quite frankly, surprised even me: "Look," I told her honestly, "I want you to understand something—I don't expect you to be perfect."

She responded as though I had splashed her face with cool water on a hot day. "Oh," she replied, putting her hand on her forehead in relief. "You don't know how much freedom you just gave me."

Those of us who are "perfectionists" are a walking mystery—a living, breathing contradiction of sorts. Though we long to experience perfection, we only seem able to focus on that which is imperfect, overlooking everything that is right and beautiful. Every "minor" flaw becomes "major," no matter how insignificant it might truly be.

When I think back on the many years when my self-inflicted compulsions drove me and everyone else crazy, I can still hear my wife's oft-repeated refrain, "Daryl, I can't believe you're making such a big fuss over this."

The "I'm Not Appreciated" Dungeon

In addition to the paradox of trying to enforce impossible standards, there is another trap perfectionists sometimes fall into—the dungeon of "they don't appreciate me enough." The entrance to this dark hole seems harmless enough, but those who have fallen into it know that it is an ever-descending spiral that ultimately plunges its victims into deep bitterness and despair.

First, we enter the dungeon by believing that someone we know—our spouse, children, customer, or business partner—doesn't appreciate us enough, or even at all; or perhaps they failed to recognize all we have done for them. We try to climb out of the abyss by telling ourselves how absolutely wonderful we've been. But, of course, that doesn't really satisfy, and we begin to slip even deeper. Next we try to "fish" for recognition from the person, or (when all else fails) argue them into appreciating all we've done. After all, it's only fair that they recognize who we are and how much we have contributed to their well-being.

When our best efforts to get their appreciation continue to fall on deaf ears, we finally end up at the bottom of that dark, lonely pit, where we languish in ever-growing self-pity, anger, and resentment. When and if we manage to climb out, the entire experience is added to our catalog of woes committed against us, ready to be remembered and used the next time we venture into the darkness.

Though God has graciously and miraculously begun a process of liberation from this recurring trap, I vividly remember what an endless cycle of bondage and bitterness it became until the power of God's acceptance set me free from looking to others for my wholeness.

Worn Out Toys

Perfectionism drives many of us into another bondage—we acquire more things, more symbols of success, more "big boy's toys." Then we become saddled with the stress of trying to protect and preserve everything we've accumulated.

"No! You can't borrow that! You might break it."

"Don't walk there. It's just been vacuumed."

"No, don't wear that! It's mine, and it's brand new."

As I mentioned earlier, my perfectionism was often tweaked by my daughter Kim's inclination for hospitality. One evening she happily announced that she had invited the entire church high school group—80 kids or more—to our home for fun and singing. The thought alone threw me into overdrive!

"What about our new carpet?" I demanded. "How are you going to keep those kids from spilling something on it?"

Kim promised they would be careful; but that wasn't good enough. I pressed her even more.

"Don't serve Coke or Pepsi. You know the stains they leave. Serve Seven-Up—it won't show the spills. Are they going to be inside or outside? They need to stay in or out. I don't want 80 kids tracking dirt back and forth from the outside."

Fortunately, Sherryl was there to save the day. When she saw that I was becoming more and more uptight, she quietly pulled me aside and said, "Even if they do spill something on the carpet, we can just have it cleaned. After all, *if we're not going to use this home for our kids and for the Lord, why do we have it?*"

Once again, the Lord used her words to expose my old ways and my need for more of God's "new" character. Over time the Lord has used her wise words to give me an entirely new set of desires for my family.

- I don't want my kids to leave home and begin their own homes remembering my gods.
- I no longer want to teach about the true and living God on Sunday and worship materialistic false gods the rest of the week.
- I no longer want to become stressed over things life really isn't about.
- I no longer want to die with everything I have in perfect condition (what an ugly, awful thought). Today I want what "toys" I possess worn out for God.

Dust is Enough—in Christ

The journey that began at Dave's bed has continued to bring an ever-widening circle of peace. It has, as I have already shared, continued to transform my entire being—how I view myself; what I expect of others; my relationships at home and at work; even my leadership style as a business owner.

This peace is built on three basic truths from the Word of God:

• **God says we're only dust.**

> *"For He Himself knows our frame; He is mindful*
> that *we are but dust."*
> Psalm 103:14

Pride tells us that we are, could, or should be better than dust. But when we begin to actually *believe* what God said—that we are miserably human—we begin to experience freedom from chasing after a lie that keeps us continually unhappy.

• **God says we're totally acceptable to Him because of Christ's death.**

> *"Therefore having been justified by faith, we have*
> *peace with God through our Lord Jesus Christ.*
> Romans 5:1

Pride repeatedly tells us we are acceptable only when we've performed in a way we believe would "please God." This drives us to keep trying harder, working harder, worrying harder. But when we believe God and trust Him to change us instead of listening to our pride, we begin to *do our best because we are free, instead of doing our best in order to become free.*

• **God says we can't please everyone.**

> *"If we say that we have no sin, we are deceiving*
> *ourselves, and the truth is not in us."*
> 1 John 1:8

Pride tells us we have to deny or hide our faults, otherwise we will lose respect and credibility. However, when we finally believe what God says and begin to admit and confess our sins to Him instead of denying they exist, criticism can only help rather than hurt. *Through Jesus Christ* we already have respect and credibility with God.

The more we grow in understanding these truths, the more thankful we become for all Christ has done and is doing for us. Apart from the wonderful freedoms He has given, we would still be trapped in defensiveness, trying to do within ourselves that which is impossible—to become perfect.

Perfection Not Required

Some years ago, on one of our family vacations, one of us coined the term "gomering" to describe anyone who made one of a broad range of clumsy mistakes. During a fishing trip a few years later, I experienced yet another occasion to thank God for the down-to-earth freedom from the pain of "gomering."

My dad and I were fishing on a lake with little luck when, late in the day, his fishing rod doubled up under the stress of a real monster! He fought the fish, playing it a long time to tire it out, while I watched and waited nervously with the net. When the fish—a huge brown

> **Life consisteth not in never "gomering."**

trout— finally surfaced, I gasped at its size (10 pounds or more) and silently prayed, "Please, Lord, help us (me) land this fish." But no sooner had I breathed that prayer than, so fast I didn't even know what had happened, I "gomered" the net job—and the monster trout was gone.

Dead silence followed. Then my father graciously said, "It was just a fish. At least we got to see him, and we're still having a good time anyway." But I still felt like crying. No, I felt like dying. Even worse than the pain of losing "the world's biggest fish" was the humiliation of messing up in front of my dad. My failure was so obvious I couldn't even try to hide behind excuses. All I could do was stare into the empty net. After a few minutes, that seemed like hours, however, I heard a small gentle voice inside that seemed to say, "Life consisteth not in never gomering." As I accepted what the Lord was saying, it was as if someone pulled the plug on all the anguish I was feeling. In a matter of minutes the "loss" drained out of me, and I began to thank the Lord for another practical freedom: I don't even have to be a perfect netter!

Losing Is A Prerequisite

For many years I considered the word "leadership"— whether it applied to parenting, teaching a class, leading a business, or whatever—to be synonymous with "being perfect," or at least nearly perfect. Leadership meant achieving and maintaining through disciplined self-effort a higher level of performance than anyone else, and then asking others to follow. Any mistakes or shortcomings should be covered over and kept to one's self. I believe this misconception explains why just hearing the word "lead" is accepted as a challenge by only a few, and results in fear and feelings of inferiority for most.

But are successful "leaders" really those who are better than anyone else? Do they really have the ability to walk on a higher road, constantly living closer than anyone

> **Losers make the best leaders.**

else to the standard of perfection? Or are the finest leaders, parents, managers, and teachers those who, while committed to do their best, understand human imperfection in God's terms, realizing what Christ has done with all of their failures, and then walking accordingly?

The way I view my own faults greatly influences the way I respond to others when they make mistakes. As long as I believed that I shouldn't or (worse yet) couldn't be wrong, I was extremely intolerant of those I led. I would nag and criticize everyone, believing my criticism would make them try harder. I didn't realize I was only producing more fear, frustration, and failure because I was imposing my impossible goals on them. In addition, as long as I believed mistakes by anyone under my leadership demeaned me and my own value, I saw each shortcoming of my family or employees as an exposure and indictment of my own failure. This caused me to criticize and condemn them even more for making me look bad. In short, as long as I believed my acceptance by others was based on performance, I was never able to see any of my own efforts, or those of people in my charge, as acceptable.

Freedom began to emerge as I discovered that Paul said only "losers"—that is, those who first *realize they lose just as much as anyone else* in God's eyes—can have the compassion and understanding necessary to provide godly leadership and encouragement to others.

*"Dear brothers, if a Christian is overcome by some sin, you who are godly should gently and humbly help him back onto the right path, **remembering that next time it might be one of you who is in the wrong.**"*
Galatians 6:1 (TLB)

God's instruction concerning losing and leadership did not end there. In the Psalms David clearly implied that we can be leaders in grace only when we accept what the Lord has done with our own failures.

> *"He has not dealt with us according to our sins*
> *. . . as far as the east is from the west, so far has He*
> *removed our transgressions* [our losing] *from us."*
> Psalm 103:10-12

So, by God's definition, "losers" are those of us who, despite an earnest desire to live for God, recognize that we will always make mistakes, and that in God's eyes we are just as imperfect as everyone else. We believe that no matter how hard we strive for excellence, we will still disappoint others from time to time because, even at our very best, we are only dust. Just as important, we also realize and believe that as we confess our failures to God, He has totally forgiven all our "losing."

This was driven home to me several years ago when we decided to make a major change in our computer system at the home office. We were exceeding our old system's capacity, and a new system would provide several critical support services to our franchises across the country. But for the first 18 months of the conversion, the system was a mess. It seemed the harder we tried, the more snarled the operation became. Soon, a number of managers began expressing their concern. What hurt the most was the feeling that my credibility was on the line. I was doing my best, but as a service organization we were still falling short.

> **When my best is no longer good enough, I can still be okay.**

One evening as I was pondering the weight of "the computer mess," of letting my associates down, of carrying the embarrassment of a poor performance, and of being disappointed in what I was and wasn't able to do, I heard a still, familiar voice say, *"I died to save you because you can't be good enough—at anything!"*

I realized I had taken my eyes off what the Lord had done for me and was focusing on my circumstances. But as soon as I realized my acceptability to God has nothing to do with how well our computer worked or how well I could please others, my pain was replaced with peace.

For most of my life I believed I needed to be "perfect" to be happy. Today, however, I am thankful that God has allowed me to discover one of the greatest liberties of all: when my best is no longer good enough, I can still be okay!

"For it is from God alone that you have your life through Christ Jesus. He showed us God's plan of salvation; **He was the one who made us acceptable to God;** *He made us pure and holy and gave Himself to purchase our salvation."*

1 Corinthians 1:30 (TLB)

"I will rejoice greatly in the Lord, my soul will exult in my God; For He has clothed me with garments of salvation, **He has wrapped me with a robe of righteousness."**

Isaiah 61:10

I Could Forgive If . . .

Why is it so hard to forgive? I've tried and tried, but that offense, inconvenience, or lack of respect just seems to live on and on in my mind, and keeps me feeling angry and resentful. I could forgive if my offender would just change enough to deserve it—or at least say they're sorry. But they won't or don't, and that fuels my feelings even more.

Do I remain critical and bitter all my life? That's a real possibility, considering how long I've already felt this way. Or is there a way to do what I haven't been able to do yet: forgive?

God says my ability to forgive grows out of recalling how much more He's forgiven me.

"*For he who lacks these qualities is blind or short-sighted, **having forgotten his purification** from his former sins.*"

2 Peter 1:9

When I think back and remember the huge offenses God has forgiven me, I discover the freedom to forgive others their "little" offenses now.

—D.K.

10

Road Blocks

Freedom to Forgive

"He who is forgiven little, loves little."
Luke 7:47

One evening at home my two sons got into an argument after school. Their verbal jousting started out tame enough, but soon it escalated in emotion and volume, and continued on far longer than it should have. After a while it broke off and the two combatants went their separate ways. Nothing had been resolved by all the shouting.

Several hours later, I was watching the evening news when I overhead one son walk into the kitchen and address the other. Of course, I was all ears—as inconspicuously as possible—to overhear what he would say.

He began with hesitation, "I . . . um . . . I need to tell you something . . . ."

I leaned forward in my chair, bowed my head, and waited for what—from the tone of his voice—I sensed was coming.

"I . . . uh . . . I'm sorry for what I said," he admitted with a tinge of agony.

I quietly thanked the Lord for this miracle. It was the first time I had ever heard my son say "I'm sorry" to anyone.

As my two boys were reconciled that evening, I couldn't help but remember one of the wonderful freedoms God has taught me along the way: *it is okay to say, "I'm sorry."* In fact, once again I've realized that God in His grace can use even my failures to glorify Himself.

Angry for Whose Sake?

The enemy of our souls will try to destroy our lives by confusing us about the right and wrong use of anger. Some Christians excuse their anger toward others by saying, "Jesus got mad in the temple, so it must be okay for me to get mad." It is easy from there to spiritualize and justify all of our personal anger as "righteous anger." However, look at how often Scripture tells us not to be angry:

> *"Now the deeds of the flesh are evident, which are: immorality, impurity, sensuality, idolatry, sorcery, enmities, strife, jealousy, outbursts of **anger**, disputes, dissensions, factions,"*
>
> Galatians 5:19-20

> *"This you know, my beloved brethren. But let everyone be quick to hear, slow to speak and slow to*

134

anger; for the anger of man does not achieve the righteousness of God. "

James 1:19-20

"Cease from anger, and forsake wrath; Do not fret, it leads only to evil doing. "

Psalm 37:8

"For I am afraid that perhaps when I come I may find you to be not what I wish and may be found by you to be not what you wish; that perhaps there may be strife, jealousy, angry tempers, disputes, slanders, gossip, arrogance, disturbances. "

2 Corinthians 12:20

The more we study this issue, the more God removes years of confusion, unhappiness, and deep-seated resentment. The anger in these verses referred to an emotion that arises from that which offends us personally: being inconvenienced, mistreated, criticized, exploited, deceived, insulted, whatever. James 1:20 makes this clear by speaking of "the anger of man," referring to the anger of our flesh. By contrast, the anger of Jesus arose only out of that which offended God. Once we understand that difference, we have no problem recognizing that we have exercised far more unrighteous (self-centered) anger than righteous (God-centered) anger.

> **Anger is believing Satan instead of God.**

Unrighteous anger actually involves allowing ourselves to be angry for Satan's sake. The "anger of man" cannot achieve the righteousness of God for a number of reasons:

135

• It keeps us angry toward those whom God loves and tolerant toward the sin God hates.

• It keeps us in the position of blaming others for our problems instead of maturing in Christlike character because of them.

• It keeps us believing more in the sovereignty of man (that others are in control of our lives) than in the sovereignty of God.

In short, anger keeps us believing Satan rather than God.

Is It Worth It?

It's easy for us to let our emotions ride the waves of our circumstances—to get angry when we're inconvenienced, upset when we hear criticism, offended when we feel we've been slighted or wronged. But is it worth it? What if, before giving in to our human anger, we would consider the consequences:

• *Is this worth hurting my family?* Those who live with us are the real victims of our stress, anger, and critical spirit.

• *Is this worth losing my respect?* If we haven't learned how to keep our cool in the heat, who will want to learn anything from us?

• *Is this worth losing my testimony for Christ?* How we react to problems can completely void the Christlike life and ministry we say we're living for.

• *Is this worth losing my health?* There's simply nothing worth accomplishing if, in the process, I allow my anger to destroy me.

Freedom From Bitterness

God revealed to me that for years I had held deep grudges within my heart—resentment toward those who failed to give me the respect I felt I deserved, who criticized me unjustifiably, who were insensitive in ways I thought were inexcusable, or whom I felt had taken advantage of me.

Because I had resolved to stop trying to get back at them, I thought I had forgiven them. But I was taken aback by God's Word when I learned that His idea of forgiveness means harboring no ill feelings whatsoever. In fact, it means to feel, act, and relate to our offenders just as if an offense had never occurred.

> "... love *overlooks* *insults*."
> Proverbs 10:12 (TLB)

> "*For I will forgive their wickedness **and will remember their sins no more**."
> Jeremiah 31:34 (NIV)

It was with deep dismay that I realized that I had never truly forgiven anyone that had offended me! I knew this was true, because merely the thought of certain people caused me to feel bitterness and resentment.

I began to pray, "Lord, I desperately want to overlook their offenses and experience true forgiveness, but how can I get rid of my bad feelings?"

God led me to Ephesians 2:11-18, where Paul seemed to be dealing with the very same problem. There he wrote about some proud Jewish Christians who were feeling critical toward uncircumcised Gentile Christians. They were saying, "Look at us. We obey God's law; but you Gentiles don't."

I realized that anytime I was critical of someone or held a grudge toward them, I was guilty of that same attitude of superiority. My critical spirit toward another person had to begin with an assumption that I was better than they were and would never do what they were doing.

Further in the text Paul wrote that the hard feelings between the two groups was the result of disagreement over God's Law. How in the world could believing Jews and Gentiles resent each other over that which is God's perfect standard of holiness?

The Bible says the Law was given to show how much we all fall short of God's holiness.

*"Now do you see it? No one can ever be made right in God's sight by doing what the law commands. For the more we know of God's laws, the clearer it becomes that we aren't obeying them; **his laws serve only to make us see that we are sinners.**"*

Romans 3:20 (TLB)

Since the Law was not given as the means of achieving God's acceptance, it certainly wasn't intended to be the performance basis for two Christian groups' acceptance of each other. Jews and Gentiles had remained enemies following their acceptance of Christ because they continued to judge each other in light of a perfect standard—God's Law. As long as they did that, the Law continued to expose how far short of perfection they actually were.

> **I had never truly forgiven anyone that had offended me.**

This leads to another great light: as long as our basis for accepting or rejecting others is how well they measure up to any standard, we (and they) will never be free to be

138

friendly and forgiving. If we continue to imagine the "law" of our selfish expectations and then judge others by how close or how far away from it they live, we can never truly accept them because they will always miss the mark—and so will we.

Truth That Unites

But if the Law divides, what really unites believers and makes us feel love toward someone we haven't even been able to like? Paul answers that very question as he continues:

> *"By abolishing in His flesh the enmity, which is the Law of commandments contained in ordinances, that in Himself He might make the two into one new man, thus establishing peace."*
>
> Ephesians 2:15 (NASB)

Paul said it was something Christ did concerning the Law (God's perfect standard) that now enabled people who had previously not liked each other to now feel friendly toward each other. But what was it that Christ did?

> *"Do not think that I have come to abolish the Law or the Prophets; I have not come to abolish them **but to fulfill them.**"*
>
> Matthew 5:17 (NIV)

God's righteous standard still exists. God will always be God; and Christ's life will always be a picture of holiness. This passage in Matthew, however, shows that Christ came not to do away with the Law, but to do away with the Law's requirements of us—*for God's acceptance of us—by fulfilling the Law in our place.*

But what specifically did it mean for Christ to fulfill God's Law for us? The Law has said we shouldn't lie, cheat, be selfish or proud, commit adultery, lose patience, worry, etc. What we begin to understand becomes a liberating light that exceeds all others: *No matter how guilty we may be of any or all of these things, Jesus Christ has presented us to God just as if we had never done any of them!*

Because Christ has fulfilled the Law in our place, we stand justified before God and accepted by Him just as if we were never selfish, never lied, never lost patience—never failed with our kids, never had any pride, never failed in our marriages, never did anything wrong!

This freedom of freedoms exceeds every other emotional "high" I've ever known. I can describe my wedding day and the birth of my first child with words like "ecstatic," "happy," and "joyous." But there are no words to describe my heart's response to what Christ has done for me.

> *"For Christ Himself is our way of peace."*
> Ephesians 2:14 (TLB)

Feeling Friendly Toward My Enemy

God has accepted us unconditionally because of what Christ has done for us. But how can we rid ourselves of bad feelings toward others?

> *"For He Himself is our peace, who made both groups into one, and broke down the barrier of the dividing wall, by abolishing in His flesh the enmity, which*

*is the Law of commandments contained in ordinances,
that in Himself He might make the two into one new
man, thus establishing peace."*

Ephesians 2:14-16

Christ wants to bring two "enemies" together through their acceptance of what He has done for them. So when we accept the reality that Christ has fulfilled all the Law for *anyone and everyone* who has placed personal faith in Him, there's no more "law" or basis for our criticism of them. Jesus has completely eliminated the standard they are failing to meet; therefore we no longer have

> **No matter how guilty we are, Jesus Christ has presented us to God just as if we had never sinned!**

any basis for holding their failures, insensitivity, unkindness, or selfishness against them. Christ has presented them in every way pure to God, just as He has done the same for us.

The day I began to view those things I didn't like in others from an understanding that Christ has made up for their failures, I began to feel friendly and accepting toward them. *Knowing Christ has completed me gives me a feeling of peace with Him; and believing Christ has done the same for others gives me a feeling of peace toward them.*

Freedom to Keep Forgiving

Soon this wonderful truth gave me the freedom to forgive some long-lasting grudges and to truly feel friendly toward some "prickly pears" I'd never before been able to embrace. But the feeling didn't last forever. In time, some of those old attitudes began to reappear. My first concern was, "Didn't I get the victory I thought I had?"

That's when God, in His goodness, directed me to the verse I needed to know and believe in order to experience His freedom on a daily basis:

> *"Brotherly kindness, and in your brotherly kindness, love. . . . For he who lacks these qualities is blind or short-sighted, **having forgotten his purification from his former sins.**"*
>
> *2 Peter 1:7-9*

If we are finding it hard to forgive and love someone again, we've forgotten just how much Christ has forgiven us. So

> **Remembering all Christ has forgiven us gives us the freedom to forgive one another.**

the freedom to forgive never begins by considering the merits of the offender, but by remembering the extent to which Christ has forgiven us.

Love Avoids No One

> *"If someone says, 'I love God,' and hates his brother, he is a liar; for the one who does not love his brother whom he has seen, cannot love God whom he has not seen."*
>
> *1 John 4:20*

According to this verse, from God's perspective we exercise only one of two attitudes toward others; either hate or love—there's no middle ground.

"Hate" doesn't just refer to negative attitudes but also to the absence of thoughts and feelings of love. Avoiding or ignoring someone is painful to anyone, and that's part of "hateful" activities. We may try to excuse this kind of hate by saying, "I don't really dislike them, I just don't have anything in common with them." God's forgiveness does not reject anyone (though someone may reject His forgiveness).

> *"There is a saying, 'Love your friends and hate your enemies.' But I say: Love your enemies! . . . If you love only those who love you, what good is that? Even scoundrels do that much. If you are friendly only to your friends, how are you different from anyone else? Even the heathen do that."*
>
> Matthew 5:43-47 (TLB)

Remember:

- Returning evil for evil is evil.
- Returning good for good is human.
- Returning love for evil is Christlike.

One of the greatest barometers of our walk with the Lord is our feelings toward those who otherwise seem unlovely and are difficult to be with. *God's love avoids no one.*

Purpose in Life

Today as I remember that God's primary purpose for my life is to continually change my character into more Christlikeness, I'm learning to view every person I talk to as the tool God may use to do just that. If my next human encounter is a complaining customer, instead of reacting to defend my performance, I see the importance of first asking the Lord, "What do You want to teach me through this criticism?"

I've developed an increasing familiarity with several of His replies: "humble you," "teach you patience," "give you greater appreciation for my gift of holiness," "grow your faith," and "increase your love for those you feel don't love you!"

It's interesting to see how, when my primary purpose is Christlikeness, criticism can actually become my friend. As I ask the Lord to continue to change me, I find my old resentful attitudes toward an accuser or one who inconveniences me replaced with appreciation for what the Lord has taught me through them.

—D.K.

11

Chains Required

Freedom to Hear What Hurts

*"The ear that **hears the reproof** of life will abide among the wise."*

Proverbs 15:31 (NIV)

We had spent several great weeks together as a family—swimming, water skiing, and fishing at Lake Shasta in California. Before returning home we decided to travel north to British Columbia to visit my brother, see the city of Vancouver, and take my two sons on their first-ever salmon fishing trip.

The first evening of our trip back home, we stopped for a fish dinner and leisurely reminisced about the highlights of our vacation—two big fish, the shops in Vancouver, all the laughing and fun together. That's when I noticed that my youngest son—only 10-years-old at the time—had tears in his eyes. As I watched, he began to sob, trying to hide his face behind the menu. Then he started weeping so hard he could barely speak.

I asked him what was wrong, but he wouldn't tell us. Instead, he kept crying harder and harder, at times even choking and gasping for air. Finally, when I told him we needed to know what was wrong or we would have to leave dinner and take him to a hospital to make sure he was okay, he began to speak.

Between deep sobs, sighs, and gasps for breath, he explained his distress. "Remember when all of you were calling me 'picks' (short for 'toothpicks' because of his thin-looking legs while on water skis) up at the lake?" he asked. We knew exactly what he was talking about. "Well, while we were up at Uncle Gerry's, I looked at my legs in his mirror—and they really are skinnier than anyone else's. And all this time I've been laughing on the outside, my heart has been sagging and sagging on the inside, until now . . . it's finally broken." Then he began to cry again, even louder than before.

Hearing that we had broken our youngest son's heart, broke our hearts as parents and put the rest of the family in tears. The grand finale of our family vacation, a formal fish dinner, was totally overshadowed by something far more important as we apologized again and again to Doug, telling him how deeply sorry we were. We had no idea the damage we had done, and we certainly hadn't meant to hurt his feelings. Could he ever forgive us?

"Please, Doug," we asked again and again, "will you forgive us?"

Of course, he said he would, and he did. But even more significant, right in the midst of that crisis, God graciously gave me another insight. There in the restaurant I vowed to

Him and to my family that I would never again refer to any physical characteristics in nicknaming or teasing my children—or anyone else. The hurt I felt after breaking my boy's heart was as bad as any pain I'd ever experienced. But along with the tears I shed because of the hurt I had caused him, I found myself weeping tears of joy over the light-giving reproof God had just brought into my life.

At the time, I had no idea how significant this God-sent lesson would be. But years later the lesson I learned from my son's pain would protect me from making the same mistake with my daughter—which in itself became another lesson in the goodness of God's reproof.

Our youngest daughter, who was five years old at the time, was beginning to lose her "baby fat" and take on a more slender look. As it became increasingly difficult to hold all of her in my lap, I caught myself calling her "my little spider girl." I had no idea then that she would go through several years during her teens when—even though we considered her tall, thin, and beautiful—she would think she was ugly. Had I, her father, continued to reinforce her sensitivity and fear by calling her a "spider girl," I would have broken her heart just like I had broken my son's. Wonderfully, through my son's honest words, God in His goodness dealt with my insensitivity before that could happen.

It's Okay to Be Wrong

Several years later, after our oldest son had started working for our company, he came home grumbling because he had to wear our business uniform shirt on the job.

> It's even "successful" to admit we're wrong.

"Dad," he complained, "where did you get those *ugly* shirts?"

149

Now it just so happened that those "ugly shirts" were my pride and joy. I had worked with one of my vice-presidents to design and create the outfits for all our employees to wear as a statement of our pride, service quality, and uniformity across the nation. So my first thought was to defend our "designer" apparel and ask my young upstart what he knew about company image and uniforms.

But then I sensed a reminder of something I had recently learned: *It's okay to be wrong.* I stopped and asked God to renew that truth. I had no sooner prayed then I felt my defensiveness drain out. I realized that the person talking to me represented the general age group of the majority of people our company was requiring to wear those shirts. It seemed only logical to reply, "Okay—how about you designing a new line of clothing—something that you and others your age would be proud to wear?" Once he got over the shock of my suggestion, he willingly agreed.

Today—ten years later—I am amazed at the annual increases in the volume of our apparel sales. It's a direct result of offering a design that more people want to wear. I'm learning it's not only okay, but at times it's even "successful," to admit we're wrong.

The Benefits of a Complaint

Although I've tried my best for more than fifty years to avoid them, some complaints still seem predestined to find their way to me. More often than I would like, I've been reminded that I still don't have it totally together in my family, my business, or even my personal life. The fact that the

> **The best of dust is still dust.**

complaints I heard were often well-deserved only frustrated and angered me further—until I discovered that the Lord said that this is the way it will be all our lives. Why? Because, as we've already seen in Psalm 103:14, *"We are but dust."*

Even when we try our hardest we will still fail because *even the best of our dust is still dust*. Moreover, others will always find some fault with us and complain because they, too, are made of the same stuff—dust!

Once I made peace with the fact that I couldn't eliminate all the complaints from my life, my curiosity began to grow. If I can't escape them, how can I benefit from them? Over the years I've learned this about complaints—they can:

• Build character and foster patience, non-defensive attentiveness, honesty, and—if necessary—my apology.

• Clarify precisely what I must do or can do to satisfy the one making the complaint.

• Cause me to deal with any anger I might feel toward my accuser.

• Give me the benefit of a warning before I lose a customer or, more important, a relationship.

• Provide an opportunity through my response and commitment to improve whatever is necessary.

• Move me closer to the Lord to understand how, once I've done my best, to experience peace in the face of complaints.

• Make me return again and again to Galatians 6:4, until I understand and apply the difference between unattainable perfection and my attainable best effort.

• Cause me to realize that more godliness is required to live and deal with complaints than to live without any complaints at all.

Born To Be Defensive

But how, once we understand all of this, can our initial response to complaints still be defensive? Where does that defensiveness come from? God's Word says that we were all born to be defensive, because we were born with pride:

> *"For all that is in the world, the lust of the flesh and the lust of the eyes and the boastful **pride of life**, is not from the Father, but is from the world."*
> 1 John 2:16

Pride continues to build up our ego by telling us that we're good. When that happens, we perceive any criticism or complaints as unjustly tearing us down, telling us that we're no good. That is enough to make any of us, in our own way, retaliate.

Throughout the Bible, God's message is one that pride does not like to hear:

> *"We are all infected and impure with sin. When we put on our prized robes of righteousness **we find they are but filthy rags**. Like autumn leaves we fade, wither and fall. And our sins, like the wind, sweep us away."*
> Isaiah 64:6 (TLB)

This stands in stark contrast to what our pride wants us to believe. However, *when we believe what God says—that there's nothing good in us—instead of believing our pride, then there's nothing left for criticism to tear down.* This enables us to view complaints as opportunities for growth rather than as personal attacks.

Criticism Is Our Friend

How can criticism be a friend when it never feels friendly? It's always felt like an enemy because it demeans and

> # How can something that hurts so badly be a friend?

embarrasses us. Furthermore, it only appears to say that we're still disappointing others when we had hoped to be beyond that point in life by now. That's why we often blame the critics. Surely they misunderstood. They didn't have all the facts. And who are they to criticize, anyway.

But now we're supposed to believe that criticism is good company for me? How can something that hurts so badly be a friend? Solomon said:

> *"He whose ear listens to the life-giving reproof will dwell among the wise... And before honor* [respect] *comes humility* [willingness to hear where we're wrong]*."*
> Proverbs 15:31-33

So if "reproof" *(corrective criticism)* is a source of information to us that is "life-giving" *(not life-taking)*, and if accepting it *(instead of being defensive)* will cause us to "dwell among the wise," and if "honor" *(respect versus disrespect)* results from it—isn't criticism a friend?

Truth Seeking

In recent years, I've experienced the growing, multi-faceted benefits of listening to criticism rather than reacting against it. As I continue to realize that God's first purpose in all my circumstances is to make me more like Him, He continues to transform my old defensiveness into "truth seeking." This principle means setting aside *who* is voicing the criticism (even if they don't like me), and *how* it is being said (even if they are angry), and with an open heart asking the Lord, "Do You have some special life-giving reproof for me in what is being said?" Obviously not everything we hear is from the Lord. That's why we need His wisdom as we listen to criticism.

Success From Complaints

Complaints, quite frankly, have cost me some good business over the years; but those same words have also taught me how to *keep* a whole lot more. In fact, I really don't know how I would be where I am today without them. Some of the greatest freedoms in my life have emerged as God revealed His "truth" through criticisms and complaints.

The Bible says that criticism—*reproof, rebuke, comment, assessment, review*—is an integral part of the success of our life and our vocation (see Proverbs 15:31-33). To confirm this we need only stop for a moment to consider just a few of the changes we've made because of them. Here are several complaints *I've* received that I value as priceless today:

• From my wife: *"Do you want your kids* (and employees) *to think they can never please you?"*
• From a company manager: *"I think the corporate recognition program stinks. A whole lot of us have worked just as hard all year but only one gets the credit."*
• From God's Word: *"Your message is 'grace' but your lifestyle is 'Law.' Because you still feel the need to appear perfect, you continue to expect it of everyone else."*
• From a manager's wife: *"Daryl, you help our husbands build their businesses but not their marriages. Isn't that just as important?"*
• From my son: *"All the time you've been teasing me about my skinny legs, I've been laughing on the outside*

but crying on the inside. "

Complaints can serve us as marriage, family, business, and personal reputation savers. I thank God for them!

"Poverty and shame will come to him who disdains correction, But he who regards a rebuke will be honored."

Proverbs 13:18 (NKJV)

Money Talks

Money talks. Have you ever heard its voice? Those of us who have know that just listening to it makes us miserable, resentful, and critical. What's worse, believing what we hear when dollars talk can cost us our respect, integrity, and entire life's ministry.

Here are just a few things I've heard money say over the years:

- *"You're worth more than you're getting."*
- *"They're getting too much."*
- *"Always look like you have lots."*
- *"Cheating isn't really cheating if others are doing it."*
- *"More money would solve all your problems."*
- *"Wrong becomes right if it is necessary in order to compete."*
- *"You deserve it all."*
- *"Breaking your word is OK if what you agreed to isn't."*
- *"Loopholes are opportunities to get more."*

—D.K.

12

The Fast Lane

Freedom from Believing More Will Make Me Happy

*"But those who want to get rich fall into temptation
and a snare."*

1 Timothy 6:9

I asked my oldest son one day, "If I were to say to you the two words: 'more money,' what would be the first thing that comes to your mind?"

Without hesitating he replied, "More freedom."

I asked him to explain his meaning.

"More money," he said, "means less stress in paying my bills. It would mean my wife wouldn't have to work. It would mean evenings free and more time for fun."

His line of thinking seemed to make sense on the surface, but as we discussed it further, we both arrived

> ## A higher salary will not produce greater liberty.

at this question: *If absolute freedom requires more money, wouldn't God give it to all believers right now?*

Is Making Money Godly?

Several years earlier, I had begun to search the Scriptures for answers concerning the same issue. I didn't see how a total commitment to the Lord could be compatible with money issues like sales, budgets, and profits. And even if I were to stay in business, how could I ever be settled on such questions as how much money is "right" to earn, and how much is "right" to keep? As I started my search I discovered this passage:

> *"The one who looks intently at the perfect law of liberty . . . shall be blessed in his deed."*
> James 1:25 (NKJV)

This verse doesn't promise freedom as a result of looking intently at the "perfect salary of liberty," the "perfect sales commission of liberty," or the "perfect profit of liberty"—which is where I looked for freedom for most of my life. This verse also says nothing about how little or how much a person makes or has; it only says that perfect freedom is found by looking intently at God's Word.

The next verse I came across was initially troubling:

> *"Come now, you rich, weep and howl for your miseries which are coming upon you."*
> James 5:1 (NKJV)

Reading this I wondered, "Who are these rich types? Am I included? Does 'rich' refer to anyone who owns their own business? What size home or how much money in the bank qualifies someone as 'rich'?"

For the moment I concluded that regardless of the meaning, I—as well as most—could live one step below his or her current standard and still survive. Couldn't most of us live in a house or apartment with one less room; give up one dress or pair of pants; give up a pair of shoes and maybe even one car, and still live?

In light of all those among the world's five billion people who are destitute, couldn't anyone who has food to eat and clothes to wear possibly fall under the biblical category of "rich"? And, if so, is owning an extra change of clothes, or several pairs of shoes, or even a second car really wrong?

Several years ago I had the privilege of visiting India with my oldest daughter. Because I planned a special trip for each of my children as they graduated from high school, she had asked if she could go with me to India to see firsthand the country, the people, and the missionary work in which I was involved.

India is a country that is home to one-fifth of the world's population, all contained within a land area one-third the size of the United States. The majority of India's people live in abject poverty. I don't mean in houses with only one room; I mean in only one room that has a cow dung floor and four walls, or in no room at all. I don't mean with only one pair of shoes; I mean sandals or no shoes.

As we were taking off from the New Delhi airport, after

161

two weeks of touring the country together, I turned to Kim and asked, "What will you remember most about our trip?"

Without hesitation she said, "The love for the Lord among the Christians I met."

I asked her why that was the first thing that came to her mind. "Don't you see that in the U.S.?" I asked.

"I've never seen at home what I've seen here," she said. "I don't see it in the lives of my friends, not even in the people in my Sunday school class."

"Why do you think those Indian Christians appear to love God more?" I asked.

"I think," she said, "it's because *they have nothing else to love.*"

Who Are the Rich?

As I continued probing, I discovered that the "rich" refers to someone—regardless of how much they have or don't have—anytime they're driven to get more; compelled by greed instead of godly character; and when the primary drum beat inside their head is for more money, possessions, and things.

> *"But those who **want to get rich** fall into temptation and a snare and many foolish and harmful desires which plunge men into ruin and destruction."*
> 1 Timothy 6:9

Material things in themselves are not condemned, nor is diligence. It is the wanting, the having to have more, the craving for something else, that God says will ruin and destroy our lives and the lives of those around us. Diligence as a Christian means applying oneself seriously to the responsibilities we've always had—budgets, planning, policy, procedures—but with a desire, first and foremost, for Christlike character instead of personal achievement.

So how do we avoid becoming the one who always wants more?

> *"But flee from these things, you man of God; and pursue righteousness, godliness, faith, love, perseverance and gentleness."*
> 1 Timothy 6:11

The word "flee" means to denounce these thoughts and in prayer and meditation on God's Word run as fast as we can away from this temptation. If we think *more* will bring us *more freedom*, we're to immediately get on our knees in our hearts and ask God to replace the desire for more things with a desire to be more like Him.

I can well understand Timothy's emphasis on running. My endless pursuit of "more" in order to gain more security, more peace, and more happiness was the very thing that added stress and ruin to my life and to others' lives as

> **Diligence: performing my responsibilities with a greater desire for attaining Christlike character than mere material achievement or fame.**

well. When "more" was my focus, not having it made me aloof, mentally consumed, and perpetually irritable. It caused me to be harsh and quick-tempered toward any family members who got in the way of my enslaved pursuits. I didn't have time to talk to my wife. I wasn't interested in my kids' interests. When I was home, my mind was still out trying to protect what I had and figuring out how to get more. And, as I've already said, enough was never enough.

How Much Is Godly?

So how much money is godly? James says that when "more" is our passion, we will fall into temptation. He warns that one of those temptations is being dishonest in order to get "more."

> *"Behold, the pay of the laborers who mowed your fields, and which has been withheld by you, cries out against you; and the outcry of those who did the harvesting has reached the ears of the Lord of Sabaoth."*
> James 5:4

It is easy to become deceived in our thinking concerning what is fair, equitable, honest, and considerate of others. In fact, without even realizing it, we can cheat those closest to us because the *"more"* god blinds us to what's fair and honest in what we get and how we get it.

The flesh's temptation to cheat was graphically illustrated to me several years ago as I was negotiating to purchase a good used car (which now resides in a junk yard). I was sitting in the seller's home, exchanging a check for the pink slip, when —after he had received my check and signed off on the car— the seller said, "You know you have to pay six and a half percent sales tax on this sale. And I have to send in a bill of sale and note how much you paid. So, how much do you want me to put down?"

Immediately my mind entertained a fleeting thought: "The tax authorities will never know." But then, because of God's continuing work in my life, the next thought that entered my mind was, "God *will* know." I had never cared before; but now I did. And I knew I didn't ever want to go back to the weight of feeling it's all up to me.

After a few moments of silent deliberation I told the seller, "The amount I paid."

"Seven thousand dollars?" he asked. "Are you sure?"

"Yes," I said. "I'm sure."

"Wait a minute," he said. "You want to pay six and half percent sales tax on the entire seven thousand dollars?"

"No," I replied. "But seven thousand dollars is what I paid."

As I've already mentioned, I used to think that whatever I could get away with short of putting a gun to someone's head was "just good business." Even worse, I thought it was what I had to do to be successful, particularly in a world where everyone else seems to be doing the same thing.

But then I read Jeremiah 22:13:

"Woe to him who builds his house without righteousness and his upper rooms without justice"

God said it is "woe" to me if I gain more (save the six percent sales tax, for example) dishonestly.

"More" in Our Relationships

The Scriptures show us what God desires in our relationship to money and possessions:

"Do things in such a way that everyone can see you are honest clear through."
Romans 12:17 (TLB)

A new perspective on honesty brings with it convictions

> # Success is not measured in dollars and cents.

that are 180 degrees from what the world believes—like not trying to profit personally from others' mistakes; or advising sales clerks when they don't charge enough; or not trying to put a good look on a bad used car by putting the good spare tire on the front and the bald one in the trunk and parking it so the worst scratches don't show.

James added murder to the charges against those who were reaping dishonest gain.

> *"You have condemned and put to death the righteous."*
>
> James 5:6

The Bible is saying that murder is the ultimate extent to which the desire to get "more" could take a person. At first I assumed this verse couldn't apply to *me*. While understanding murder is a temptation that can go hand-in-hand with dishonest gain, I told myself I'd never kill anyone to get more of anything. But then I wondered, "What am I doing to my children when I've taught them that financial success at any price is the most important thing in life? What am I doing to them when, by my example, I've said money and material achievement are more important to me than they are? I'm destroying them in the same way."

For most of my life, an insatiable appetite for "more" motivated everything I did. Though I would have held myself up as being exceptionally honest, fair, and considerate, looking back in the light of my new understanding I realized the false idol of greed and materialism will never allow nor produce the fruit of true righteousness. Its outcome will always be death to me as well as others. Only when the "more" god is put to death will the genuine fruit of God's righteousness begin to appear.

Remarkably, as the desire for more gives way to the Spirit of God, I have found that people become more important than things, and relationships take priority over material gain. In God's economy, success is not measured in dollars and cents, but in how much or how little my words, actions, and behavior toward other people are a reflection of who He is.

What Is Fair?

As we long for God to take away our appetites for "more," it is amazing the new values that begin to appear. We ask ourselves what true honesty is instead of assuming we're already honest. We defend our integrity whenever it is challenged.

> **Freedom from the compulsion for more allows character to become more important than accomplishment.**

How does God measure intangibles like integrity, consideration, and honor? What is His concept of fairness as opposed to ours or that of the world we operate in? And how might that truth affect not only the way we think but also the way we act?

A growing freedom from the inner compulsion to achieve and accumulate more allows character to become more important than accomplishment. As God replaces the desire for material gain with a desire for character gain, we experience changes He wants to make in our business and professional life.

> *"You slave owners* [business managers] *must be just and fair to all your slaves* [employees]. *Always remember that you too have a Master in heaven who is closely watching you."*
>
> Colossians 4:1 (TLB)

For example, today I see how unfair it was for me to assign to each of my own responsibilities a priority of 1 to 10 while leaving my employees to assume that everything I ever asked of them was a 10. Even worse, I understood how wrong it was to perpetually expect more and more of them without ever considering the emotional and physical toll my demands might be taking.

My unfair expectations really came home to me as I tried to imagine what life must have been like for a member of my staff. What would it be like to feel that every responsibility assigned me was a 10; that every task carried a job-security level of importance; that nothing could wait or slip; and still I was expected to do *more*? I finally understood why some of my employees lived with more stress, worked longer hours, and enjoyed their jobs even less than I did. As an employer, I strove to make my work as reasonable as possible, but it was never as important to do the same for my employees. Since they were being paid, the stress resulting from my requests was their problem, not mine.

Now I consider it a high priority to regularly review each of my staff's workload. I want to understand their comfort level in regard to responsibilities, special requests, authority, interruptions, training, equipment, my availability, and their freedom to share any concern. Today, the thought of sacrificing lives and families is repulsive to me; and even though it's been a long road, *I can't enjoy my job unless I know my employees enjoy theirs.*

What Do You Think?

*"Where there is no guidance, the people fall,
but in abundance of counselors there is victory."*
Proverbs 11:14

I've discovered one of the greatest weaknesses of my former leadership style was the failure to create a freedom for others to be honest with me—at any time, on any subject. The tunnel vision created by my pursuit of material success alienated me from the counsel of others. I was so focused on what I wanted that any other input was either irrelevant or insignificant. Moreover, in my narrow heart and mind, listening to the counsel of others somehow diminished my position and authority.

But as God, through His Word, continued liberating me from the "more" god, He steadily increased my desire and appreciation for input from those around me. The benefits of this miraculous change astound me today. For example, in our corporate headquarters this freedom is the main reason we enjoy an ongoing working unity among our staff, a growing team tenure, and respectful relationships with our franchisees. It encourages a critical mutual evaluation process for all company policy. Everyone's honest view helps assure the accuracy, integrity, and right perception of all we do. Most important, everyone's honesty helps filter out the bias and humanness in all of us.

Freedom for candid expression has become our staff's unifying bond. Instead of just "going along" with or rubber-stamping the company's purpose, policies, and decisions, we have become unified in our common belief in what we are doing.

This openness within our day-to-day operation has increased the importance of certain principles. If I were to summarize these outworkings of God's freedom, they would include:

- Believe that there's wisdom in the counsel of many. As I mentioned earlier, I used to believe it was my responsibility to have all the answers, and that I would lose the respect of my "followers" if I didn't. Today I believe just the opposite.
- Never be defensive. I want my employees to know that I am not only receptive to hear, but that I *desire* to hear, different opinions as well as critical things about either me or the company.
- Respect every comment and question. Show verbal appreciation for a person's willingness to share *anything*.
- Express a desire for regular, honest communication.
- Initiate the discussion on particularly stressful subjects, such as wages, workload, relationships, promotions, or whatever.
- Stress that open, honest communication will always make their relationship with me more secure, not less secure. Others' willingness to share honestly with me—particularly when I know it's difficult for them—will be their greatest asset.

New Values for the Same People

Recently, while reflecting on my staff, the years we have spent working together, our anticipated future growth, and the new personnel we will need, I asked myself what—assuming they had the capability to do their jobs—I desired most in my employees. I was surprised at the contrast between my values now and what I would have preferred before the Lord began changing my heart.

Twenty years ago I would have listed the following as most important:

(1) *Productivity* (how much my employees could accomplish);

(2) *Quality* (how few mistakes they would make); and

(3) *Profitability* (how much income they could generate).

Today, the first thoughts that come to mind (which quite frankly, produce the best of those qualities listed above) are:

(1) *Honesty*,
(2) *Teachability*, and
(3) *Brotherly Love*.

The reason these are what I desire most in my staff is because these are what I desire most for myself.

Honesty

> *"Oh Lord, who may abide in Thy tent ? . . . He who walks with integrity, And works righteousness, and speaks truth in his heart."*
> Psalm 15:1-2

As we ask God to help us understand what honesty means in day-to-day relationships, we no longer feel the freedom to say one thing and think another, or to just say what "sells." He gives us a growing desire for all our conversation to be compatible with what He sees as true in our hearts. He teaches us to desire and highly value complete honesty from others with us and with each other. This includes, specifically:

- Telling others what we really believe instead of saying what we think they want to hear.
- Saying "I'm confused" if we are instead of nodding in agreement.
- Admitting our mistakes instead of trying to avoid responsibility for them.
- Saying "I don't know" if we don't, instead of feeling compelled to give some answer.
- Never exaggerating a concern in order to better prove our point.
- Saying "I need to leave early to see my son's game" if that's the truth, instead of saying, "I need to run some errands."
- Telling the truth instead of something else to avoid hurting someone's feelings.
- Never interfering or allowing the listener to believe something different than what we know is true.

Teachability

"A wise man is hungry for truth."
Proverbs 15:14 (TLB)

For many years it was easy to think of myself as teachable, until, in the light of this verse, I began to look for actual evidence of that trait. I discovered that if I am sincerely hungry for truth, these characteristics will be evident and growing in my life:

- Constantly inviting input from others about how I can improve instead of seeking compliments for the way I am.

172

- Frequently saying "I'm sorry" and "I was wrong."
- Being easy to talk to, especially concerning a criticism or recommendation.
- Not being defensive when others express their opinions or disagreements.
- Appreciating any and all suggestions and points of view.
- Seeking to maintain many counselors.

Brotherly Love

"Don't be selfish; don't live to make a good impression on others. Be humble, thinking of others as better than yourself. Don't just think about your own affairs, but be interested in others, too, and in what they are doing."

Philippians 2:3-4 (TLB)

It is amazing how incredibly practical and productive God's Word is in all walks of life. "Brotherly love," as the Bible defines it, is a critical ingredient in the cohesiveness and productivity of any organization. This includes a growing desire to:

- Be sensitive to the responsibilities, needs, and stresses of all staff and employees.
- View others' efforts and contributions as important as our own.
- Always think and speak respectfully of all others.
- Be quick to initiate a resolution to a conflict, whether it be work or personality-related.

- Deal kindly with all people.
- Extend help and encouragement rather than criticism in the face of others' shortcomings.
- Look more to give credit than to take credit.
- Never assume we can do someone else's job better than they can.

God treasures the immaterial over the material. He continually liberates us to seek Him rather than seeking things. What infinite satisfaction and reward there is in desiring more of the ***true God*** instead of desiring more of the ***"more" god***.

"Blessed are those who hunger and thirst for righteousness, for they shall be satisfied."
Matthew 5:6

The Mid-life Myth

The way the so-called "mid-life crisis" is written and talked about these days, added to the many people who say they have one, it might seem like we have no choice but to have one too. But do we have a choice?

It's true that aging continues to take its toll on our ability to maintain clarity of mind, physical strength, and personal stamina. It's also a fact that age changes our appearance as our weight shifts and we discover wrinkles where we once were smooth. But these things do not necessitate a "crisis" — at least not for those who genuinely believe that:

- *God has given us total, permanent, and unconditional value in His eyes—value that simply cannot deteriorate with age (see Ephesians 1:18).*

- *Aging in this life means we're drawing closer to eternity and an infinitely better life in God's kingdom (see Ecclesiastes 3:11).*

- *God works all our past mistakes together for His and our future good (see Romans 8:28).*

- *Our life's purpose is to "walk humbly before God." We can do that just as well at 70 as we could at 30 (see Micah 6:8).*

—D.K.

13

The Rear-View Mirror

Freedom from Regret

"Who is the man who fears the Lord? ... his soul will abide in prosperity."

Psalm 25:12-13

Really No Regrets ... Ever?

Looking back over the past 30 years, I see a paradox. On one hand, I see a life of human failures, many of which I've already shared. On the other, I've watched in awe as God has taken those very shortcomings and supernaturally transformed them into that which glorifies Him — not me — today. Though I consider the person I was and the things I did as a pile of worthless rubble, God has shown me that He can resurrect from my worst that which ultimately brings glory to Himself. After all, if He—as God—is sovereign,

He ultimately is in absolute control not only over my future, but over my past as well. So while in one sense I have ample reason for regret, I rejoice in God's marvelous grace that covers all my failures and resurrects new life from the ashes. Isn't that real freedom?

> *"And we know that God causes all things* [including all past failures] *to work together for good to those who love God, to those who are called according to His purpose."*
>
> Romans 8:28

What Is God's "Prosperity"?

It may sound odd at first hearing, but the "prosperity" God's Word talks about is not necessarily the opposite of "poverty." If it were, only the rich could experience the blessings promised to those who fear the Lord.

"Prosperity" promised to all who seek Him most often is best understood as the opposite of "regret." In the book of Joshua, the Lord said to His servant:

> *"This book of the law shall not depart from your mouth, but you shall meditate on it day and night, so that you may be careful to do according to all that is written in it; for then you will make your way prosperous, and then you will have success."*
>
> Joshua 1:8

In the Psalms, David said of the "prosperous" man:

> *"His delight is in the law of the Lord, and in His law he meditates day and night. And he will be like a*

tree firmly planted by streams of water, which yields its fruit in its season, and its leaf does not wither; and in whatever he does, he prospers."

Psalm 1:2-3

The first time I read the above passages, I wondered, "Just what is this 'prosperity'? If I give my life to the Lord and remain obedient to His Word, what will happen to me and to my family? How does God's promise to bless me with success relate to my job or my business? And perhaps more important, how will I feel about my life when I'm 40, 50, even 60 years old? Will I feel fulfilled? Or will I wish I could somehow go back and live my life all over?"

As I sought to understand this, I began to realize that God's "prosperity" includes many blessings, one of which is His special enabling to begin making right decisions in life—choices that, because they are sourced in His eternal Word rather than our limited intelligence, produce eternal value and lasting fulfillment rather than regret. It's the opportunity to go in submission to the

> **God enables us to make life choices that produce eternal value and lasting fulfillment.**

Scriptures and in prayer before God, seeking the decisions He would make if He walked in our shoes—whether to accept certain responsibilities; how strong a stand to take with our children regarding some matter of discipline; whether we should move our family or make a career change; whether a decision or action will improve compatibility with our mate or affect our kids' respect for us.

"Who is the man who fears [obeys, respects, reverences] *the Lord? He will* [not 'He might'] *instruct him in the way he should choose."*

Psalm 25:12

179

> *"The steps of a man are* [not 'may be']
> *established by the Lord."*
>
> Psalm 37:23

> *"He shows how to distinguish right from wrong*
> [not 'He leaves us in a fog of options'], *how to find the*
> *right decision every time* [not 'sometimes']. *"*
>
> Proverbs 2:9 (TLB)

In the Valley of Decision

I could literally fill a book with stories of how God has clearly made known to me what I should do on numerous occasions through a proper understanding of His Word, a desire that grows out of time spent in prayer over a particular matter, and the counsel of my wife and others. But here I would like to share just two:

One evening one of my teenagers came home with an obvious "distilled" smell which, frankly, surprised my wife and me. My first thought was, "Not my kid! This can't be true. This can't be happening in our family. Where have I failed?" My next concern was, "This could destroy my kid's life. What should I do? I've never dealt with this before. Should I just sit back and conclude that as teens they're now old enough to make their own choices? Or should I take a firm stand, running the risk of making them angry and driving them to do something even worse? Will they run away in the middle of the night to do only God knows what? *What should I do?"*

After much prayer with Sherryl—both of us often in tears—and the Lord leading us to read what He says about the responsibility of a father for the discipline and upbringing of his children, and His promise in return, it became increasingly clear what I should do.

> *"Discipline your son . . .while there is hope . . . ."*
> Proverbs 19:18a (TLB)

> *"Foolishness is bound up in the heart of a child; the rod of discipline will remove it far from him* [not drive him away].*"*
> Proverbs 22:15

From these verses, I began to realize that my actions should not be based on fear of what my teenager's response might be to me, but on what my response should be to God and His Word. The Scriptures I read gave me the freedom of knowing first that I was being obedient to God and thus could trust Him with the outcome. Second, Proverbs 22:15 gave me the freedom of knowing that doing what I had to do would ultimately accomplish God's best (not my worst fears) for my child.

After several days of prayer and discussion with my wife, I shared with my teenager the decision God had put on our hearts. I said, "You can't do this any longer and live here. I believe what you're doing is not honoring to the Lord and can potentially destroy your life. I

> **Doing what God says will accomplish God's best for my children.**

love you enough to let you hate me for a while if that's what it means to not give you the freedom to make a harmful choice that could produce a lifetime of bad consequences. "

As difficult as it was to deliver that kind of ultimatum with every intention of following through, God had caused me to realize that my kids' future happiness was too important not to do everything within my power to see that they experienced it.

Several years ago, that adult child—now married—thanked me for the strong stand I had taken back then.

"Dad," he said, "I want to thank you for your firm decision because it gave me the backbone I needed at the time to say no to my friends. When they wanted me to drink with them, I was able to tell them that I couldn't because I wouldn't be able to live at home if I did."

Although this situation turned out well, no matter how my son might have responded to my discipline, I will never have to regret doing the wrong thing—because circumstances are not God's measure of a correct or incorrect decision. I'm grateful, of course, that he responded positively. But my fulfillment today doesn't come from looking at what my decisions, or for that matter, my life has or hasn't accomplished. It comes from simply knowing I've been obedient to what I understand from God's Word.

> *"Obey my voice and I will be your God and you will be my people, and you [Daryl] will walk in all the way which I command you, that it may be well with you."*
> Jeremiah 7:23

While God leads us through prayer and His Word, He also directs us by placing His desires in our hearts and minds.

> *"Delight yourself in the Lord and He will give you the desires of your heart."*
> Psalm 37:4

> *"I did not tell anyone what my God was putting into my mind to do."*
> Nehemiah 2:12

Several years ago the lease on our office building was up for renewal, and because it was the safe, easy thing to do, I was planning to sign another 10 year commitment. Not long before, however, I had hired a new controller for our company. After only two weeks on the job (and just before I signed a new lease) he came to me and said, "Daryl, I hear you're thinking about signing another long-term lease. Why don't you consider building your own office building?"

I immediately rejected the idea. "No way," I said. "I had a 'build my own' experience 22 years ago that ended up taking more than two years, and my wife and I had to move twice in the process. I'll never do that again."

But—and in hindsight I'm convinced it's because God brought that particular controller to us—he ignored my response and over the next few days asked me a second and third time. So I paused and reasoned, "Lord, You sent me this controller after much prayer and many interviews. Are You telling me through him to construct an office building of our own?"

As I continued pondering this issue before the Lord, I became increasingly open to the possibility this might be what He wanted me to do. On the surface, the timing seemed all wrong. The U.S. was on the verge of war with Iraq and the press was predicting that the price of oil was going to go up to $100 a barrel. There were signs of a deep recession, possibly even depression. But as time went on, God not only seemed to be directing me through my controller's advice, He began taking away my fear, planting a seed of desire in my heart, and continually opening otherwise closed doors. So we tentatively moved ahead with a plan to build.

As we proceeded with the financing for construction, my initial fears returned a bit when the day came to sign all the loan papers. Part of me wondered if I was making the biggest mistake of my life. But then God's Spirit brought to mind the many verses that assure me that if I'm totally submitted to Him, He *is* leading me.

> *"Since the Lord is directing our steps, why try to understand everything that happens along the way?"*
> Proverbs 20:24 (TLB)

Today, the building God directed us to build has become uniquely suited in so many ways to our purpose. In retrospect I can see that signing that lease—a perfectly acceptable option to me at the time—would not have been nearly as beneficial as the plan He had in mind.

Now, to be sure, I don't always discover an immediate answer for every question or concern. But I've learned that if I continue to lay a situation before the Lord in prayer, He

> **God's will first concerns what He wants to do in our lives, not with our lives.**

will—in His time—make His direction clear. He always has. My greatest concern is that I not become so consumed with what I think should happen that I fail to remain patient and sensitive to His leading. Too often I think I need an answer "now" when God actually wants to teach me to wait on Him.

> *"Rest in the Lord and wait patiently for Him."*
> Psalm 37:7

We need to remember that God's direction always first concerns what He wants to do *in* our lives rather than *with* our lives; what He wants to direct and develop in our character.

184

So in times when God's leading regarding some circumstance has been clear for a while, but then *seems* as though He's "hung up the phone," it's always possible that He is directing us to what's most important of all.

"And without faith it is impossible to please Him."
Hebrews 11:6

It's Never Too Late

When I think of regret, I can't help but be reminded of the disappointment and anguish we often see on the faces of those who have dedicated their entire lives to one goal or achievement, but then have fallen short. Whether at the World Series, the Super Bowl, or the Indy 500, competitors have been known to break down in sobs and tears of regret in the face of failure and disappointment, which is surely understandable. Often their remorse is not only over failing at a lifelong goal, but also over "wasting" the many years they spent preparing for success that never came, with no way to reclaim those years.

In much the same way, countless people have been driven to chronic depression and worse by failure and disappointment in their careers. Parents, too, have been faced with horrible depression and remorse because of the choices they and their children have made. And in all of these situations, regret can rule the heart and mind through a hopeless desire that the past as well as the present could somehow be changed.

But in a miraculous, merciful, and wonderful contrast, Jesus Christ offers a life without remorse, the opportunity to place one's heart in His hands *at any time*, knowing from that point on that His direction is sure, and that He will redeem the past in a way that brings glory to Himself.

Looking back, even at times when it seemed far too late for God to make anything good out of something worthless I had done or been, I can see His incredible transformation of that "too late" situation. One of the most meaningful of those experiences occurred one day not too many years ago as I was sitting in my office. My youngest son walked in and said, "Dad, can I talk to you for a few minutes?"

"Sure," I said. "Sit down."

"Dad," he said. "I want to ask you something important, okay?"

I nodded.

"Uh . . . Dad . . . I'm really serious, okay?"

I nodded again, my curiosity definitely aroused.

Clearing his throat he continued, "Dad, I want to ask you to be the best man in my wedding."

I was stunned. My first thought was, "Did he really say what I thought he said? This can't be!"

Finally I replied, "You don't know how much I appreciate your asking me. But you really need to ask someone more your age. In fact, you need to ask whoever it is you consider to be your best friend."

Doug cleared his throat again. "But Dad," he said, "I consider you to be my best friend."

That's when I thought, "Not me. Surely not me!"

This was the son that for many years of conflict I used to criticize the most. Our competitive natures kept us at odds, neither of us wanting to lose at anything—sports, games, even discussions. In those days of arguing, disrespect, and

> **Thank You, Lord, that it's never too late to begin loving You!**

hard feelings, I could not have imagined the time would come when Doug would consider *me* to be his best friend. But the work of God's love in both our lives had torn down those walls of alienation.

Too emotional to verbally respond, and with tears in my eyes, I turned my heart to the One who not too long before had become *my* Best Friend. I said again to Him, "Thank You, Lord, for giving me, even late in life, this priceless respect and friendship of my son. Thank You, Lord, for healing the past so that I don't have to live forever in regret."

> *"Then I will make up to you for the years that the swarming locust has eaten."*
> Joel 2:25

> *"And your eyes will see this and you will say, 'The Lord be magnified beyond the border of Israel. A son honors his father.'"*
> Malachi 1:5-6

Really Believing

Is it possible to be so familiar with certain Scripture verses that we can think we believe them, when in fact we may not? For example, a friend recently shared with me, "I know God forgives me, but I still feel so guilty. I guess I'm just having a hard time forgiving myself."

I wonder, is it possible to still feel guilty (assuming there is no unconfessed sin) and really believe verses like Psalm 103:12, Jeremiah 31:34, and Romans 5:1? Though many times in the past I struggled with this situation myself, I don't think it's really possible. God tenderly brought me to the point where I had to ask myself, "Where does God ever say that after we accept Christ's forgiveness we still need to forgive ourselves?" He doesn't. The focus of God's Word is never on what we still need to do for ourselves to "feel" forgiven; rather, it's on really believing what Christ has already—and perfectly—done for us.

—D.K.

14

Freeways

Living Free

"Where the Spirit of the Lord is, there is liberty."
2 Corinthians 3:17

The Great Freedom of the Gospel

After more than 50 years of observing the frailty of my own human nature, I believe two of the most destructive wrong attitudes in life are inferiority and superiority. Inferiority makes us feel rejected by God and insecure with others. Superiority makes us feel less needy of God and more critical of others. Until we accept what God has to say about both of these, they rob us of His freedom.

Some of us struggle for years with feelings of inferiority as a result of comparing our shortcomings and pasts with what we perceive to be good in others. We grow up believing we're not as good, we've made worse mistakes, we don't have the same potential, we are less deserving.

At other times in our lives, perhaps without even realizing it, we might harbor attitudes of superiority which cause us to believe we're better, that our sin is not as

> **Inferiority and superiority destroy.**

black, that we walk closer to God and are therefore "better Christians." This can be as obvious as a "holier than thou" attitude or as subtle as a critical spirit.

Based on my own experience, I believe it's possible for any of us to feel inferior in some areas—such as parenting or spirituality—while considering ourselves superior in others— such as career or academic achievement.

The gospel exposes the truth about both of these self-destructive attitudes, which will ultimately prevent us from ever *really* experiencing liberty in Christ.

First, the Bible says we're all equally bad, that none of us has a leg up on anyone in terms of meriting God's acceptance:

> *"Our prized robes of righteousness . . . are but filthy rags."*
>
> Isaiah 64:6 (TLB)

However, the Word also says in 2 Corinthians 5:21, that all in Jesus Christ are equally "righteous."

> *"He made Him who knew no sin to be sin on our behalf that we might become the righteousness of God in Him."*

God doesn't even see us in *shades* of white. Rather, through Christ's death we're all declared "white-white," or perfectly cleansed. God looks upon us as righteous not because of what we do or how we perform, but because that which Christ did 2,000 years ago is effectual for us *today.*

Therefore, when we believe the gospel—which declares that all of us are equally bad but also *equally righteous* in Christ—we feel *accepted* by God and *secure*, or free, with others.

It is this righteousness in Christ—God's declaration that we are 100 percent acceptable to Him *right now*—that forms the foundation for everything else we will ever experience in our relationship with Him. Until we understand and believe this, we will spend our lives wondering and worrying about His acceptance of us instead of living in the joy of what He has already and completely done for us.

The Chief of Sinners

For some, the Bible, Jesus, and salvation primarily has to do with eternity, not with daily life. But as we continue to study God's Word, we discover that everything we know about our eternity with Him and all that He guarantees about our future is made possible because He has declared us "righteous" *right now.* In addition to our guarantee of eternity in heaven, God's gift of righteousness is a gift of freedom for *today.*

> *"Therefore having been justified by faith, **we have*** [present tense] *peace with God through our Lord Jesus Christ."*
>
> Romans 5:1

193

> *"For if by the transgression of the one, death reigned through the one, much more those who receive the abundance of grace and of the gift of righteousness will reign in life through the One, Jesus Christ."*
> Romans 5:17

But even as *I* began to understand this, I did not experience the liberty God intends because my attitude of superiority was blinding me. It was telling me that I was fairly okay—hard driving . . . achieving . . . "serving the Lord." As long as I continued valuing myself "more highly than I ought to think," putting confidence in my own abilities, I could never appreciate the magnitude of what Christ actually did for me.

One day, as I was talking with one of my sons about God's love, I drew a line and wrote on it the numbers one through ten. I then asked him to put an "x" on the line—ten being best—to indicate how much he felt his mother's love. He marked "ten." Then I asked him to indicate how much he felt God's love—and he marked a "two." When I asked him why he'd marked only a "two" for God, he thought for a few minutes and said, "I guess it's because I don't feel I've ever been that bad."

Amazingly, those had been my past sentiments. Why? At that time at least some who knew me viewed me as a model Christian. I had no offensive habits like swearing or getting drunk. I served on my church's board of elders; held Bible classes for my employees; and, in general, thought of myself as honest and truthful. Now, if I had killed someone, I could see how God's forgiveness would have meant a lot. But having grown up in a Christian home, avoiding what I believed were "the big sins," my limited understanding of God's forgiveness left me feeling that He had not done much that really affected my life in this world. God's forgiveness was something that would affect me after I died (I hoped), but it just didn't seem to have much relevance before then. (It seems awful today, but I believe this is an outlook some of us fortunate enough to have been raised in Christian homes have experienced.)

Then, in my studies I came to the sixth chapter of Proverbs and saw something I have not forgotten to this day. God lists seven sins He hates; the third is murder—*the first is pride.* Realizing God lists pride before murder hit me like a sledgehammer as I began to admit to myself that I had pride *on top of pride.* I had an insatiable appetite to be liked and respected. I didn't want to be wrong or corrected. I wanted things my way and was quick to become defensive. I even wanted the credit for introducing others to the Lord!

As I realized I was consumed with the first sin God hates, I was overwhelmed by a sense that *I am*, as Paul said, "the chief of sinners." To now understand that God has nevertheless chosen me to receive His gift of righteousness in spite of my wretched unworthiness, caused my feeling of God's love to go off the scale.

Though it's certainly an inadequate example in comparison to the eternal kingdom, it helps me to imagine someone coming along at a point in time and paying off the mortgage on my home, giving me clear title. If someone actually did that, how would I feel? And what if that person was someone I had been

> **The Word lists seven sins God hates; the third is murder —the first is pride.**

hostile toward my entire life? Once I was able to overcome my doubt that this was really happening, I would be speechless . . . incredulous . . . totally unable to express my gratitude! I'd probably tell everyone I knew—my friends, my family, even total strangers! And I know that person's generosity and unthinkable gift would be one of the greatest memories of my life.

Paul says that Christ came along and paid off my eternal—and much deserved—destiny in hell and gave me clear title to heaven. How much greater a gift is this, and how much more valuable than clear title to a house is a clear title to heaven?

> *"And when you were dead in your transgressions and the uncircumcision of your flesh, He made you alive together with Him, having forgiven us all our transgressions, having canceled out the certificate of debt consisting of decrees against us and which was hostile to us; and He has taken it out of the way, having nailed it to the cross."*
>
> Colossians 2:13-14

Peeking Under the Sheet

One day a young woman approached my wife and me with a problem. At first she was afraid to tell us why she wanted to talk, obviously wrestling with something very big. But eventually, between sobs, she blurted out, "I had sex with three different men during my last marriage. I've since become a Christian and have asked God to forgive me. But I still feel dirty and guilty."

I stopped her before she went into any more detail and said, "You're telling me about physical adultery, which I know has produced some very painful and sad consequences. But God also speaks in terms of spiritual adultery, and I don't know of anyone who is more guilty of that than me. To be honest with you, I've been in bed with my money, my pride and my self-centered appetites for most of my life. In fact, I lived in spiritual adultery for 32 years. No one could be a worse sinner and more undeserving of God's mercy than me. But not many years ago I discovered God's great gift of righteousness."

I held up a black pen and a sheet of white Kleenex. "You feel as black as this pen, don't you?" I asked.

"Yes," she said.

I placed the white sheet over the black pen and said, "God says that when you received Christ as your Savior, He took Christ's blood and put a complete covering over you. He made your failures just as though they never occurred, so from that moment on, He sees you as white and clean in His eyes.

"The reason you still feel so guilty and dirty is because you're peeking under the 'sheet' of God's forgiveness. You're still choosing to see yourself through your eyes instead of through God's."

After we prayed together, thanking God for what He had completely done on her behalf, she left with a smile beginning to form on her face.

Not long after that conversation I was at a retreat in Southern California. I had just concluded a weekend marriage seminar and was getting into my car to leave when a woman in tears came rushing toward me, with her husband close behind. "Can I talk with you for just a few minutes?" she asked.

"Sure," I said.

Pulling back the sleeves of her blouse she showed me scars on her wrists which she had slashed three times in the past, trying to commit suicide. Her eyes red from weeping, she shared with me how she

> **Freedom is only a belief away.**

had spent more than $15,000 in therapy, only to come away as distraught as when she began. She then asked, "Can you help me?"

"No," I said, "I can't. But freedom for you is only a belief away. I *can* introduce you to the One who is Truth. Believe in Him and what He says and you'll be free."

I reached inside my car and pulled out my oft-used little black pen and white tissue and told her the same story I had shared a few weeks earlier. "This is how you feel about yourself," I began. "But Christ has covered you with His white robe and now sees you as pure and clean. You are troubled because you still choose not to believe God, and you keep looking under the sheet to see your life apart from what God says He has done for you. The day you *really* believe and choose to look at yourself as God sees you, you'll never be the same."

I then went on to share with the woman the good news that God not only forgives us, He treasures us—just the way we are today. "You see," I told her, "God values righteousness; and He infinitely values you today, not because you live righteous, but because He's imparted to you His very righteousness."

"What are the riches of the glory of His inheritance in the saints."
Ephesians 1:18

Wanting To vs. Having To

Last year a friend asked me, "Daryl, have you ever struggled with lust and thinking about sex much of the time?"

"Yes," I said, "for most of my life, in fact."

The truth was that whenever I was away from home and thought no one I knew would see me, I felt a strong attraction to the magazine racks and the pictures in so-called men's magazines. I knew I shouldn't look at them and felt guilty when I did, but there never seemed to be enough power in just *knowing* I shouldn't look to help me stop. Then, too, even in my marriage I've found myself often consumed with sexual thoughts and desires. There was a time when I wanted my wife to dress more sensually around me, and thought far more frequently about her body than her character. And, whether it was dinner or family time, my thoughts still usually carried through to the bedroom.

Then one day the Lord led me to understand that even marital sex could become my god.

> *"Therefore consider the members of your earthly body as dead to immorality, impurity, passion, evil desire, and **greed**, which amounts to idolatry."*
> Colossians 3:5

Greed, I learned, meant wanting more of *anything*—money, pleasure, even sex. Realizing I was still living for the sex god, after the Lord had convicted me concerning the "success" god, the "respect" god, and a host of others, was a new and humiliating thought.

Then I also remembered that Paul, in his letter to the Corinthians—Christians who were just like you and me, totally human, experiencing every failure we experience—nevertheless addressed them as:

> *"Saints* [holy ones]."
> 1 Corinthians 1:2

Why? Because, as he told them,

> *"You were washed . . . you were sanctified . . . you were justified in the name of the Lord Jesus Christ."*
> 1 Corinthians 6:11

As I thought about these verses, particularly in the context of the rest of Paul's letter, it seemed he was telling these Christians that if they really understood what Christ had done for them, they would not be acting the way they were—fighting, jealous of one another, lusting, and thinking about sex all the time. The power to change their lives didn't exist in just knowing what they shouldn't do, but in a greater comprehension of what Christ had already done for them. Paul knew God's mercy and grace toward us in light of our total unworthiness is so great, that when the eyes of our hearts become enlightened, we will desire to submit to Him and His Word out of a heart overflowing with love. When we understand the incredible wonder of what Christ has done for us, we will experience a growing natural desire to live a life of gratitude and surrender to Him instead of continuing to fight a losing battle against the do's and don'ts of religious rules and law. That's why he interceded for the Ephesians, and I'm sure for all Christians, *"I pray that the eyes of your heart may be enlightened"* (Ephesians 1:18a).

I can still remember getting my very first car, a free gift from my dad. I was careful to park it where it wouldn't get dinged or scratched, and I dusted it off every morning. I even watched for dirty shoes—and absolutely no french fries were allowed.

In the same way, the Bible says that when I realize I've received the free gift of a *new life* from my heavenly Father, I will respond with a hunger for cleanliness (righteousness) and will desire to keep that new life clean.

Now I must confess that for most of my life I've lived with more desire to keep my yard, my car, even my new tie clean than to keep my new life clean. Yet God still chose to declare— me?—holy? *Lord, how could you be so gracious to me, the chief of unappreciative sinners?*

There's an old Christian song I used to sing quite often in my father's home church, without any tears or emotion. But today I can't sing it without a deep stirring in my spirit.

It's my song of freedom today:

> *There is a song I love to sing*
> *I love to hear its words,*
> *They sound like music in my ears*
> *The sweetest ever heard*
> > *Oh how I love Jesus*
> > *Oh how I love Jesus*
> > *Oh how I love Jesus*
> *Because* [just look at how much] *He first loved me!*

Provisions

I am grateful for these Divine gifts that provide my freedom:

*God's Grace: My security is God's forgiveness, not my performance. God saved me because of what He did, and not because of anything He requires me to do. **This is my greatest freedom.***

*God's Word: The Scriptures continually remind me of God's ability in the midst of my difficulty. The Bible also causes me to see and deal with sin in my life instead of criticizing what I see in others. **This is my greatest encouragement.***

*My Wife: Sherryl tells me things no one else would—things that sometimes hurt, but which later mean the most. And thank God she continually reminds me that "family" is for life, just when I begin to think my business is. **She is my greatest help.***

*My Children: They still call me "Dad" when others may call me unkind things. They are the next generation of me, my home, and my values. **They are my greatest future.***

*My Ministry: I treasure every opportunity God provides to encourage others where our mops meet the floor. As long as God gives me breath, I want to introduce others to "Life." **This is my greatest privilege.***

Thank You, Lord.
Thank you, Sherryl.
Thanks, Greg, Kim, Doug, and Shelli.
Thanks, Mom and Dad.
And thanks, David.

Addendum

A sampling of excerpts from Environment Control's Employee Newsletter

Fretting

Fretting has been so common in my life it seemed to be a part of my personality. Whether it was a reaction to something that went wrong, or a matter I couldn't control, I was agitated by it.

But aren't those feelings just a normal part of life—impossible for any of us to avoid?

> *"Do not fret—it leads only to evil."*
> Psalm 37:8 (NIV)

Perhaps the reason I've been upset so often is because I've never viewed fretting as being among the "BIG" sins I should avoid, i.e., adultery, swearing, lying. And so, while fretting continues to masquerade as an innocent emotion, does it not rob me of all my peace and joy? Further, it trashes my faith, causes me to disobey God, and denies the sovereignty of God.

In our daily journey we encounter many fretting detours. The exit ramp certainly never appears evil, and places to turn around are few and far between. The only warning is in our traveling guide—the Word of God— which says fretting leads to evil.

I Got the Music in Me

I didn't realize until I started listening to several gospel tapes on my way to work, several years ago, just how much what I listened to influenced the mood of my entire day. When I listened to the news in the morning I often arrived at the office angry over an injustice or uptight about the predicted effect of the economy on business. When I listened to country-western music, I'd walk in (with a rhythm) humming the words, "swingin' doors . . . sawdust floors . . a heartache drowns. . . as the whiskey pours . . . ." Somehow those words and similar others did not seem edifying to my spirit or the spirit of those with whom I worked.

Then, one day, someone gave me a tape of John Starns singing "Rise and Be Healed" and "He Came to Me." *These* songs encouraged me to just believe God in every circumstance in life. And as I listened, tears of joy would often well up as I felt my faith once again rekindled and restored. I'd come to work BELIEVING and overjoyed in the Lord!

Diamond in the Rough

Have you ever known someone who really got on your nerves? A co-worker perhaps, or an employee or customer? I have.

Maybe you can't quite put your finger on what it is about this person that irritates you—they just do. Have you ever thought, "Is it just me, or is it really them?" If not, perhaps it's time you stopped and asked yourself that question.

Our Lord places people in our path to cause us to be molded and shaped to His image. God's Word tells us this process of shaping is a lifelong journey for the Christian, and one which we can all too often "buck" under like a horse trying to unseat its rider. You see, we are diamonds in the raw, with all sorts of rough edges that need to be polished and shined so that our lives bring glory to Him— the Master diamond cutter. If we resist His shaping, we are limiting our own potential to bring glory to God through our lives.

Now back to that irritable customer, employee, or co-worker who is about to drive you crazy. What does God want to reveal to you in this situation? He may want to teach you patience, tolerance, or unqualified love. Perhaps you require a lesson in compassion, or honesty, or self-sacrifice.

We are all destined to be diamonds.

How Many Plates Should You Spin?

Some of the most important and difficult decisions in life concern how many responsibilities we should accept. It's difficult to say "no" but often we find ourselves in more difficulty because we've said "yes." Invitations to "worthwhile" whirling are everywhere and as long as there is a shortage of spinners, plates will come begging to be spun. How many should you spin?

Here's how I determine whether or not to be involved in a project. I ask myself:

1. Is this the right thing to do? Does this responsibility fit into my life's values—is it worth the investment of my time? Bottom line, is this an ego thing, fun thing, feel-pressured-into-thing, or right thing to do?

2. Am I qualified to accept this responsibility? Do I have both the ability and capacity to do this job well? God's Word says that satisfaction in what I do is derived from how well I spin—not how many I spin. (See Galatians 6:4.)

3. Can I handle this responsibility without jeopardizing any other? Do my current dishes benefit or imperil each other? Are those I'm involved with pleased with my spinning? I can test this from time to time by asking my wife if she's happy with my "mate" plate or asking my key personnel if they're pleased with my "makin' it good" platter.

4. Do I have enough time for personal exercise and relaxation? Am I feeling good, thinking clearly, and acting rather than reacting in all of my current involvements?

5. Are my church, PTA and local charity plates balanced properly? Are they spinning like a top while my "mate" plate is wobbling?

Remember, there will always be someone asking for help with their spinning. If you're not careful, you could spend your life keeping their pottery together while your fine china lies in ruins at your feet.

More Than Billing

> *"Blessed Lord teach me your rules. I have recited*
> *your laws and rejoiced in them more than riches. "*
> Psalm 119:12-14 (TLB)

Is this verse true of us? Do we rejoice in being transparently honest in all our dealings more than we do in getting a new account? Do we think more about being content than we do about what more we deserve? And, is responding with kindness and compassion toward those who disappoint us really more important than the amount of this month's profit check?

David said knowing and living by God's Word thrilled him more than a new home, a new chariot, or an increase in his earthly kingdom. He said he repeated verses to himself more during the day than he talked about expanding his kingdom or controlling costs. And he prayed for God to make him more like Him, more than he prayed for God to bless his "business."

The bottom line for David was: *"Those who love thy law have great peace, and nothing causes them to stumble"* (Psalm 119:165).

Only Two Ways

When we hear a business acquaintance talk about saving taxes by charging certain personal expenses to his company, do we feel envious? Do we wonder, hopefully, if it's okay for us to do the same, since "most people do it"? When I realized there are only two ways to act in life—the world's way or God's way—it helped me when I was confronted with these types of "opportunities."

For example, I've often been tempted to save $3,000 tax dollars annually by reversing the charge for gardening between my home (the greater amount) and office. However, what used to be justification—"everyone does it"—has become a huge, red flag. I've learned that what the majority of people do is the world's way. God's way is to make me different—"light"—to the darkness all around. That "light" includes being honest no matter how unfair the tax law may seem and trusting Him to care for me instead of Uncle Sam.

Handling income and expenses honestly may be different than most, but that's a good sign. Actually, that's a God sign!

Good Stewards of Who We Are

Do you ever wish you were different from the way you are? Do you wish you had a different personality, or different abilities from those you have?

But, does God have the same wish for you?

> *"Thus says the Lord who made you and formed you from the womb."*
> Isaiah 44:2

Do you become discouraged because you can't increase your sales or manage your business as well as someone else? Again, what does God say?

> *"Let everyone be sure that he is doing his very best, for then, he will have the personal satisfaction of work well done and won't need to compare himself with someone else."*
> Galatians 6:4 (TLB)

Never compare yourself to someone else's billing or profit. Just remain focused on being a good steward of the way God made you.

A Slave to My Attitude

I'm not the boss—my attitude is. It owns me. It takes me wherever it goes. If it dwells on the horizons of opportunity, things "worthy of praise" (Philippians 4:8) and "forgiving others" (Ephesians 4:32) that's where I live. If it camps in the valley of things worthy of criticism and "I've been inconvenienced," I go there as well.

Unfortunately, valleys are easier to coast into than mountains are to climb. Gravity alone takes us into the valley, while much effort is required to reach the top of the mountain. The slide into bitterness is slick and quick. The climb to forgiveness is steep, our footholds constructed of pride overcome.

Several giant steps in conviction are necessary to live above the downward tug of our daily difficulties. Here's three:

1. All problems are to help me grow stronger, not weaker. They are reasons for staying, never excuses for quitting. Their purpose is to reveal attitude flaws in me. (See 1 Peter 1:7; James 1:2-4.)

2. No harm or injustice exists within God's sovereign will for me. Every disappointment, inconvenience, and even loss will result in my future benefit if I love God. (See Romans 8:28.)

3. God owns my life, my family, and my business anyway.

Environment Control Building Maintenance Company
P.O. Box 2000
Hayden, ID 83835-2000
Phone: (208) 762-0700
Fax: (208) 762-1313
Internet: www.environmentcontrol.com